A Garden of Love and Healing

A Garden of Love & Healing

LIVING TRIBUTES TO THOSE WE HAVE LOVED AND LOST

Marsha Olson

Fairview Press
Minneapolis

Published by Fairview Press, 2450 Riverside Avenue, Minneapolis, MN 55454. Fairview Press is a division of Fairview Health Services, a community-focused health system providing a complete range of services, from the prevention of illness and injury to care for the most complex medical conditions. For a free catalog of Fairview Press books, call toll-free 800-544-8207, or visit our website at www.fairviewpress.org.

Library of Congress Cataloging-in-Publication Data

    Olson, Marsha, 1955–
        A garden of love and healing : living tributes to those we have loved and
lost / Marsha Olson.
          p. cm.
        ISBN 1-57749-111-4 (pbk. : alk. paper)
        1. Sanctuary gardens. 2. Gardens—Religious aspects. 3. Gardens—
Symbolic aspects. 4. Grief. I. Title
SB454.3.S25 O48 2002
712'.6—dc21
                                                        2001053205

First printing: March 2002
Printed in the United States of America
05 04 03 02   7 6 5 4 3 2 1

"Tomorrow There Will Be Flowers" by Dan Gill originally appeared in *The Times-Picayune*, and is reprinted by permission of the author.

Illustration credits: Photos on pp. XIV, 10, 54, 62, 70, 80, 94, 104 © Craig Bares, Craig Bares Photography. Photos on pp. 56, 58, 59, 64, 84, 89, 109 courtesy of the author. Photos on frontispiece, p. 86, and p. 98 by Lane Stiles. Photo on pp. 6–7 courtesy of Kay Frey. Photo on p. 9 courtesy of June L. Mucci. Photo on p. 53 courtesy of Jayne Decker. Photos on pp. 66, 67, and 68 courtesy of Lil Bromley. Photo on p. 83 courtesy of Marilyn Nelson. Photo on p. 88 courtesy of Debby Suoja Ostlund. Photo on p. 89 and p. 93 courtesy of Penny P. Moreau.

To David, Luella, and Monroe

CONTENTS

ACKNOWLEDGMENTS

Nicholas, Andrew, and Christopher—I thank you for your love, support, and patience.

Thank you, Amory, for your unending love and support. To you and Brenda and the other very special women in my life— may we continue to share our feminine gifts with each other, our loved ones, and the world.

Mom and Dad—I thank you for your quiet, steady love.

Thank you, Dan, for your encouragement.

We don't always get a chance to go back and thank those who made a difference in our lives. I want to thank three people who influenced me, although without knowing it, in developing this work: Will Reller, the chaplain at Boulder Community Hospital, who taught me, with inspiring integrity and authenticity, how to help those with hurting hearts; Jack Geer, for giving me a wonderful opportunity to work in nature and never failing to point out the beauty in the ordinary; and Cody Oreck, for intuiting and communicating to me with unmistakable sincerity that there was something that needed to be said, and done.

A very special warmhearted thank-you to these beautiful women: Nancy Lockett, June Mucci, Kay Frey, Lil Bromley, Jeanne Norton, DeeAnn Burnette-Lundquist, Jayne Decker, Debby Suoja Ostlund, Jan Weber, and Penny Moreau. You cannot imagine how much each of you touched my heart and inspired me onward.

PREFACE

As you think about creating a garden in memory of your loved one, there is something important for you to know. It is possible not only to recover from grief and loss, but to rise from its painful depths to a place of profound peace and acceptance with a completely new commitment to life and love.

Working through grief is a daunting journey, a difficult passage. It requires courage, conviction, and the faith that light *will* shine on the other side of this dark path. There is no failure in not accepting the challenge grief presents, but to refuse it may diminish your capacity to experience the richness life still has to offer. When you turn from those wounds that are asking for healing, you also turn from that place within you that knows love, compassion, and peace.

All suffering prepares the soul for vision.

Martin Buber

At the beginning of your journey, when just getting through the day is a struggle, you may feel reluctant to embrace the emotional challenge of grieving. During this time you need all the support you can get. Fortunately, support *is* available—the support of a comforting spiritual force in nature.

This gentle, soothing spiritual force surrounds and supports you like a loving mother. It is everywhere. You can experience it when you walk on a beach at the ocean. Or as you sit on a bench in a quiet courtyard. Or as you stroll through a beautiful park under an expansive blue sky. Or, as this book demonstrates, as you tend your garden.

It is my hope that this book will help those who are suffering from loss to find a sense of connection to the greater power that infuses all life and to experience a profound healing beyond that of just "getting back to normal." In a garden of love and healing, we can come to understand the paradox that, while we are of the earth, we are also part of something much, much larger.

Bread feeds the body, indeed, but flowers feed also the soul.

The Koran

My dad was a gardener. Last winter on the first anniversary of his death I was having a pretty tough time. I was walking through my yard and saw a bloom on a quince bush—one of Dad's favorites. I shared this story with one of my sisters, and she told me that at the same time she found a rose—another of Dad's favorites—blooming in winter! It made me feel like my dad was telling me he was okay.

—Jeanne Norton

1

NATURE'S HEALING SPIRIT

*G*rief evokes feelings of powerlessness, helplessness. We can do nothing to change what has happened to us. We miss what we've lost with all our being. We are paralyzed by frustration and pain.

This sense of helplessness can range from active rage to passive despair. It can be the darkest time of our life. When overcome with sorrow, our hearts tend to contract. It is an understandable, protective reflex, but this closing down diminishes our aliveness. Giving ourselves compassionate permission to mourn with an open heart is difficult; to embrace our pain makes us feel as though we will die—but we won't.

A wide variety of feelings can surface during the grieving process. Many people mistakenly believe that grief is only an emotion of sadness. While sadness may predominate, feelings of

*All
my
hurts
My
garden
spade
can heal.*

Ralph
Waldo
Emerson

longing, guilt, and anger are common as well. You may even feel relief in some circumstances. All feelings are normal. All emotions can be resolved. Emotions are energy. When you do not allow your feelings to surface, the energy becomes trapped in your body. *What you resist will persist; what you feel, you will heal.* Consciously allowing your feelings to emerge, and experiencing them fully, puts you on the path to recovery. Sometimes, it helps to focus on just one feeling at a time. To single out, acknowledge, experience, and release even one emotion is difficult but worth the effort.

Many people wonder how long grieving will—or should—take. The only appropriate answer is ... until it is finished. Mourning is considered complete when the memories of the loved one no longer evoke painful feelings of suffering and are instead replaced by a sense of acceptance. Many factors affect the resolution of grief—the age of the loved one when he or she died, the circumstances of the death, unresolved issues in a relationship, and so on. Feelings of sadness around the loss of a loved one may always be present. But the feelings can shift from suffering in sorrow and pain to a bittersweet sense of gratitude and remembrance that evokes joy. An intimate relationship with the spiritual can take you far beyond mere acceptance of your loss; it will lead you to your innermost heart where you can find the peace that surpasses understanding, the love that knows no time, place, or conditions.

A recent loss can revive feelings from past losses, even when the grief caused by those previous losses was thought to have been resolved. When you feel bad, it is not always necessary to pinpoint

Everybody needs beauty as well as bread, places to play in and pray in, where Nature may heal and cheer and give strength to body and soul alike.

John Muir

the source of the pain. Understanding involves the logical mind, the intellect, but pain is transformed through emotional acceptance. This is where the natural world comes in.

When you connect with nature, you tap into the energy of love you once shared with your loved one. This love is the balm your bruised heart needs when grieving. Nature sings a song that your heart can hear; it feeds your soul. It will, if you allow it, begin reengaging you in life. Because nature is always present, the key to connecting with it lies in relaxing, allowing, and accepting. You do not have to do a thing. Nature is available and open to all who seek it.

If you have recently lost a loved one, you may be longing for a deep connection with something pure. With a subtle shift in perception, you can find such purity within yourself and in the tender, caring spirit of nature. Allow the natural world to hold you as you move through your grief. Let your heart lead you into the garden where you can be "hooked" back into life again.

Experiencing the subtle, loving energies of the natural world is unspeakably sweet. Too often, however, we take this natural world—and life in general—for granted. The death of a loved one can make us realize how precious life is. It can push us into contact with parts of our inner selves that we have never consciously touched before. Following this thread inward can lead, paradoxically, to a deeper connection with the world at large.

We are beginning to grow in our understanding of the reciprocal relationship we have with Mother Earth. As we wake up to the negative effects we have had on the earth, we can also open ourselves to the tremendous amount of strength and nurturing

*For
every
flower
that
opens
in your
garden,
another
wound
is healed
in your
heart.*

Unknown

available in nature. And as we process our pain, we can enter into a new relationship with the earth that is ultimately healing for both the planet and ourselves. After all, it is from the earth's substances that our bodies are formed. This good mother feeds us, quenches our thirst, gives us air to breathe, and clothes and shelters us.

When I was in the depths of personal despair, I would walk for two miles every day through a nature preserve. At first, I walked at breakneck speed, only occasionally allowing my attention to wander to a flitting bird or noisy squirrel. The fast pace seemed to diffuse my body's painful energy of grief. Eventually, though, I slowed down and began to experience the purity and perfection of the natural beauty surrounding me. I began to feel a stirring deep in the core of my being. Slowly, I let down my guard against the grief I was feeling and accepted nature's gift of quiet, steady grace. This grace had been there all along; I had just been too absorbed to notice it. As my tension gradually unwound and I relaxed to the spiritual support of the natural world around me, I was gradually able to release my feelings of grief.

You, too, can open yourself to the natural spirit that enfolds and permeates life. You, too, can embrace the healing force of nature. You, too, can release your feelings of grief by creating a garden of memory as a living tribute to your lost loved one.

Many people intuitively seek refuge in gardening in times of sorrow. Gardening connects us directly with the cycle of life. A garden is itself a metaphor for life. (Life began in a garden, according to the Bible.) Gardens are vulnerable to the vagaries of climate and environment. They need loving care as they grow and mature.

He who plants a garden plants happiness.

Chinese proverb

They experience vigorous periods of growth and bloom, punctuated by quiet periods of resting and renewing.

As you tend your memorial garden and watch it change through the seasons, you will see it maturing, becoming more beautiful as the plants become stronger, fuller, and more vibrant. You will see it reflecting your own healing and the beauty of your relationship with your loved one. In time, you will be rewarded with a more tender, compassionate heart that is ready to bloom ... and love ... again.

THE DANNY THOMAS MEMORIAL GARDEN

Entertainer Danny Thomas is buried in downtown Memphis, Tennessee, next to St. Jude Children's Research Hospital, which he helped to found in 1962. The burial crypt of Thomas and his wife, Rose Marie, is situated within the Danny Thomas Memorial Garden. The garden was designed to provide a serene and soothing sanctuary for the young patients and their families. It contains more than 60 trees, including dogwoods, pines, cypress, elms, oaks, and crape myrtles; a variety of shrubs and perennials, including 82 hollies, 80 junipers, and 25 azaleas; and 45 varieties of annuals for seasonal color. Two waterfalls complete the pastoral setting.

After a loved one dies, you wonder if life will ever be normal again. Initially, resuming a normal life seems impossible—and it is impossible unless you create a new normal life that includes memories of the one who has gone, but doesn't depend on their physical presence.

My husband died very young of a chronic illness. His acceptance of his death was beyond understanding. He asked that his ashes become "part of the good earth." He died on the vernal equinox. On the summer solstice, our family planted a flowering crab tree, one he always wanted, with his ashes mixed into the roots. Our oldest son graduated from high school one year later, and we took pictures of him in his cap and gown with "Dad," who was blossoming beautifully. As long as they live, this will always be "Dad's tree."

Caring for it and watching its development substituted for the caring we had given him on this earth, and I cannot begin to tell you how it kept us all from breaking down in despair. Since then we have planted many more trees and flowers that he enjoyed, plus cultivars named "David" and fruits he loved to eat.

The sheer physical work of planting his garden was a good antidote for depression and gave us back a sense of the beauty of life. My youngest child asked me if the sun would ever shine again and feel good, and I knew how he felt. My husband's garden helped us go on the way he would have liked us to, missing him, but still keeping his influence on our lives alive. We often walk past his tree and spend a moment in reflection, prayer, and remembrance of what we promised him.

—Kay Frey

My older sister passed away from diabetes at the age of forty-three. I miss her terribly. She always said that when she got older, she wanted to sit in a rocker on the porch and paint. I found an old rocker someone had thrown out and made a planter in the seat. I decorated it with a plaque I found that said "Home is where the heart is." This year I planted impatiens and snapdragons, with vinca vine at the bottom. An old child's rake leans against it. The rocker reminds me of my sister. When I'm working or just enjoying the garden, her small section is there to give me a sense of sadness and pleasure at the same time.

—June L. Mucci

2

GIVING YOUR GARDEN MEANING

When a loved one dies, life can slip into chaos. The comfortable, normal routines of everyday living are shaken, even destroyed. You find yourself searching for meaning and understanding of what has happened. You seek answers that are not easily found.

As hard as it is to believe, however, the sun can shine again. Gardening can connect you with nature, engage your creativity, provide a physical outlet, and satisfy the psychological need for ritual to memorialize your loved one. If your loved one was cremated, it can be consoling and reassuring to scatter the ashes in your own garden.

Dedicating a space in your yard or on your patio to plant a perennial garden allows you to memorialize this special person through the loving language of flowers and plants. You can wel-

More things grow in the garden than the gardener sows.

Spanish proverb

come the essence of life back into your world. Setting up a bird-bath, birdhouse or feeder and welcoming butterflies with colorful plant blooms are further invitations to life by sharing yourself and giving back to nature.

For thousands of years, the symbolism of plants has played a significant role in human history. The Bible has references to plants; Shakespeare spoke of herbs and flowers; and the Victorians expressed what was in their hearts through flowers.

When you create a garden in remembrance, you let plants and flowers express what is in *your* heart. Through their unique language, you can symbolically honor and remember the special individual who was in your life and the loving relationship you shared.

*Y*ou don't have to have a large space to create a living memorial to a loved one. For those without the room or the ability to create an elaborate, in-ground garden, a patio or indoor pot can be planted instead. A simple potted planting can be just as meaningful as a more complex garden. Here's one suggestion: Bend a wire coat hanger into the shape of a heart, straighten the curved hook, and secure it in the potting soil. Then plant a climbing vine that you can train to grow up the wire. **Rosemary** (symbolizing *remembrance*), **English ivy** (symbolizing *friendship*), and **creeping fig** are some of the easiest and most popular plants to train into a topiary form.

Plants Representing Each Month

Choose from this list to symbolize a birthday or anniversary month.

January	carnation; snowdrop
February	violet; primrose
March	daffodil; violet
April	daisy
May	lily of the valley
June	rose
July	larkspur; water lily; sweet pea
August	gladiolus
September	aster
October	calendula; dahlia
November	chrysanthemum
December	holly; poinsettia

The Symbolism of Color

Using the language of colors in your garden, you can further reflect your loved one's personality.

White
purity and love

Yellow
intellect, optimism, good humor, wisdom

Orange
joy, confidence, independence, sociableness

Purple
intuition, idealism, self-sacrifice, inspiration, kindness, spirituality

Green
generosity, understanding, healing, humility, compassion

Red
passion, courage, spontaneity, strength, love

Blue
loyalty, affection, tranquility, patience

The Victorian Language of Flowers

The Victorians used plants to create a special language. You can use this language to add further meaning to your memory garden.

A

acacia: friendship
acacia, pink or white: elegance
acacia, yellow: secret love
acanthus: the fine arts; artifice
achillea millefolium (yarrow): war
aconite (wolfsbane; monkshood): misanthropy
adonis: painful recollections
agrimony: thankfulness; gratitude
allspice: compassion
almond: stupidity; indiscretion
almond blossom: hope
aloe: grief
alyssum: worth beyond beauty
amaranth, globe: immortality; unfading love
amaryllis: pride; timidity; splendid beauty
American cowslip: divine beauty; "You are my divinity."
American elm: patriotism
American linden: matrimony
American starwort: welcome to a stranger; cheerfulness in old age
amethyst (browallia): admiration
anemone: sickness; expectation; forsaken
angelica: inspiration
apple: temptation

apple, thorn: deceitful charms

apple blossom: preference; "Fame speaks him great and good."

apricot blossom: doubt

arborvitae: unchanging friendship; "Live for me."

arum: ardor; zeal

ash tree: grandeur

aspen tree: lamentation

asphodel: "My regrets follow you to the grave."

aster, China: variety; afterthought

auricula: painting; "Entreat me not."

auricula, scarlet: avarice

azalea: first love; temperance

baby's breath: everlasting love

bachelor's-button: celibacy

balm: sympathy; pleasantry

Balm of Gilead: cure; relief

balsam: impatience

balsam, red: "Do not touch me."

barberry: sharpness; sourness of temper

basil: hatred

basket-of-gold: calm; reconciliation

bay leaf: "I change but in death."

bay tree: glory

bay wreath: reward

bee balm: compassion; sympathy; consolation

bee orchis: industry

beech tree: prosperity

begonia: dark thoughts

belladona: silence

bellflower, pyramidal: constancy

bellflower, small white: gratitude

betony: surprise

bindweed, great: insinuation

bindweed, small: humility

birch: meekness

bittersweet nightshade: truth

black poplar: courage

blackthorn: difficulty

bladder nut tree: frivolity; amusement

blue-flowered Greek valerian: rupture

bluebell: constancy

blueberry: treachery

borage: bluntness

boxwood: stoicism

bramble: envy

branch of currants: "You please all."

branch of thorns: severity; rigor

bridal rose: happy love

broom: humility; neatness

browallia (amethyst): admiration

buckbean: calm repose

bud of white rose: heart ignorant of love

bugloss: falsehood

bulrush: indiscretion; docility

bundle of reeds: music; complaisance

burdock: importunity; "Touch me not."

buttercup: ingratitude; childishness; desire for riches

butterfly orchis: gaiety

butterfly weed: "Let me go."

cabbage: profit

cactus: warmth

camellia, red: excellence

camellia, white: loveliness

campanula: gratitude

canary grass: perseverance

candytuft: indifference

canterbury bell: acknowledgment

Cape jasmine: transport of joy; "I am too happy."

cardinal flower: distinction

carnation, pink: woman's love

carnation, red: "Alas for my poor heart."

carnation, striped: refusal

carnation, yellow: disdain

catchfly: snare

catchfly, red: youthful love

catchfly, white: betrayed

cedar: strength

cedar leaf: "I live for thee."

cedar of Lebanon: incorruptible

celandine, lesser: joys to come

centaury: delicacy

cereus: modest genius; horror

chamomile: energy in adversity

checkered fritillary: persecution

cherry blossom: good education

cherry tree, white: deception

chervil: sincerity

chestnut tree: luxury; "Do me justice."

chickweed: rendezvous

chicory: frugality

China aster: variety

China aster, double: "I share your sentiments."

China aster, single: "I will think of it."

China or Indian pink: aversion

China rose: beauty always new

Chinese chrysanthemum: cheerfulness under adversity

Chinese lantern plant (winter cherry): deception

Christmas rose: "Relieve my anxiety."

chrysanthemum, red: love

chrysanthemum, white: truth

chrysanthemum, yellow: slighted love

cilantro (coriander): hidden worth

cinquefoil: maternal affection

cistus (rockrose): popular favor

cistus, gum: "I shall die tomorrow."

citron: ill-natured beauty

clematis: mental beauty; "I love your mind."

clematis, evergreen: poverty

clover, four-leaved: "Be mine."

clover, red: industry

clover, white: "Think of me."

cloves: dignity

cobaea: gossip

colchicum: "My best days are past."

coltsfoot: "Justice shall be done."

columbine: folly

columbine, purple: resolved to win

columbine, red: anxious and trembling

convolvulus: bonds; uncertainty

convolvulus, major: extinguished hopes

convolvulus, minor: repose; night

convolvulus, pink: worth sustained by judicious and tend___ ___

coreopsis: always cheerful

coreopsis Arkansa: love at first sight

coriander (cilantro): hidden worth

corn: riches

corn bottle: delicacy

corn cockle: gentility

cornel tree: duration

cornflower: healing; felicity; delicacy

coronilla (crown vetch): "Success crow___

cowslip: pensiveness; winning grace

cowslip, American: divine beauty; "You___

cranberry: cure for heartache; hardness

crape myrtle: eloquence

creeping cereus: modest genius; horror

cress: stability; power

crocus: abuse not

crocus, saffron: mirth

crocus, spring: youthful gladness

crowfoot: ingratitude; luster

crowsbill: envy

cudweed, American: unceasing remembrance

currant: "Thy frown will kill me."

cyclamen: diffidence

cypress: death; mourning; despair

daffodil: regard

daffodil, yellow: chivalry

dahlia: instability

daisy: innocence; "I share your sentiments."

daisy, Michaelmas: farewell; afterthought

daisy, parti-colored: beauty

daisy, wild: "I will think of it."

damask rose: brilliant complexion; freshness

dandelion: oracle

daphne: glory; immortality

daphne odora: painting the lily

darnel (rye grass): vice; changeable disposition

day lily: coquetry

dead leaves: sadness

dianthus: pure love

dianthus, red: lively and pure affection

dittany of Crete: birth

dittany of Crete, white: passion

dock: patience

dogwood: durability

dried flax: utility

ebony tree: blackness

E

elder: zealousness
elm: dignity
endive: frugality
evergreen clematis: poverty
evergreen thorn: solace in adversity
everlasting: unceasing remembrance
everlasting pea: lasting pleasure

F

fennel: worthy of all praise; strength
fern: fascination
fig: argument
fig marigold: idleness
fig tree: prolific
filbert: reconciliation
fir: time
fir, Scotch: elevation
fireweed: pretension
flax: appreciation; domestic industry; fate; "I feel your kindness."
fleur-de-lis: flame; "I burn."
flowering fern: revery
flowering reed: confidence in heaven
fly orchis: error
fool's parsley: silliness
forget-me-not: true love; "Forget me not."
foxglove: insincerity
foxtail grass: insincerity
French honeysuckle: rustic beauty
French marigold: jealousy
French willow: bravery and humanity

fuchsia, scarlet: taste

Fuller's teasel: misanthropy

fumitory: spleen

furze: love for all seasons

gardenia: refinement

garland of roses: reward of virtue

gentian: "You are unjust."

geranium: gentility

geranium, dark: melancholy

geranium, ivy: bridal favor

geranium, lemon: unexpected meeting

geranium, nutmeg: expected meeting

geranium, oak-leaved: true friendship

geranium, penciled: ingenuity

geranium, scarlet: comforting; stupidity

geranium, scented: preference

geranium, silver-leaved: recall

geranium, wild: steadfast piety

germander speedwell: facility

gillyflower: bonds of affection

gladiolus: ready armed; strength of character

globe amaranth: unfading love; immortality

goat's rue: reason

goldenrod: precaution; encouragement

goldilocks: tardiness

gooseberry: anticipation

gorse: anger

gourd: extent; bulkiness

grape, wild: charity

grass: submission; utility

Guelder rose: winter; age

harebell: submission; grief

hawkweed: quick-sightedness

hawthorne: hope

hazel: reconciliation

heath: solitude

helenium: tears

heliotrope: accommodating disposition; devotion; faithfulness

hellebore: scandal; calumny

hemlock: "You will be my death."

hemp: fate

henbane: imperfection

hepatica: confidence

hibiscus: delicate beauty

holly: foresight

hollyhock: ambition; fecundity

honesty: honesty; fascination

honeysuckle: generous and devoted affection; bonds of love; sweetness of disposition

honeysuckle, coral: the color of my fate

honeysuckle, French: rustic beauty

hop: injustice

hornbeam: ornament

hortensia: "You are cold."

houseleek: vivacity; domestic industry

houstonia: content

hoya: sculpture

hundred-leaved rose: dignity of mind; pride; grace

hyacinth: sport; game; play

hyacinth, purple: sorrow

hyacinth, white: unobtrusive loveliness

hydrangea: a boaster; heartlessness

hyssop: cleanliness

ice plant: "Your looks freeze me."

Iceland moss: health

Indian Jasmine: attachment; "I attach myself to you."

Indian pink, double: always lovely

Indian plum: privation

iris: message

iris, German: flame

iris, yellow: flame of love

ivy: friendship; fidelity; marriage; faithful love; constancy

ivy, sprig of: assiduous to please

Jacob's ladder: "Come down."

Japan rose: "Beauty is your only attraction."

Japanese pear: fairies' fire

jasmine: amiability

jasmine, Cape: transport of love; "I am too happy."

jasmine, Carolina: separation

jasmine, Indian: attachment; "I attach myself to you."

jasmine, Spanish: sensuality

jasmine, yellow: grace and elegance

johnny-jump-up: happy thoughts

jonquil: "Return my affection."

Judas tree: unbelief; betrayal
juniper: succor; protection
kingcup: desire for riches; ingratitude; childishness
laburnum: forsaken; pensive beauty
lady's slipper: capriciousness; "Win me and wear me."
lagerstroemia, Indian (crape myrtle): eloquence
lamb's-ears: gentleness
lantana: rigor
larch: audacity; boldness
larkspur: lightness; levity
larkspur, pink: fickleness
larkspur, purple: haughtiness
laurel: glory
laurel, common (in flower): perfidy
laurel, ground: perseverance
laurel, mountain: ambition
lavender: distrust
leaves, dead: sadness
lemon: zest
lemon balm: sympathy, pleasantry
lemon blossom: fidelity in love
lettuce: coldheartedness
lichen: dejection; solitude
licorice, wild: "I declare against you."
lilac, field: humility
lilac, purple: first love
lilac, white: youthful innocence; youth
lily, day: coquetry

lily, imperial: majesty

lily, white: purity; sweetness; modesty; beauty

lily, yellow: falsehood; gaiety

lily of the valley: return of happiness

linden or lime tree: conjugal love

live oak: liberty

liverwort: confidence

lobelia: malevolence

locust tree: affection beyond the grave; natural change

London pride: frivolity

lotus: eloquence

lotus flower: estranged love

love-in-a-mist: perplexity

love-lies-bleeding: hopeless, not heartless

lupine: voraciousness; imagination; sorrow

lychnis: wit

madder: calumny

magnolia: dignity; love of nature

magnolia, swamp: perseverance

mallow: mildness

mallow, marsh: beneficence

mallow, Syrian: consumed by love; persuasion

mallow, Venetian: delicate beauty

manchineel tree: falsehood

mandrake: horror

maple: reserve

marigold: grief; despair; uneasiness

marigold, African: vulgar minds

marigold, French: jealousy

marigold, prophetic: prediction

marjoram: blushes

meadow saffron: "My happiest days are past."

meadowsweet: uselessness

mercury: goodness

mesembryanthemum: idleness

mezereon: desire to please

Michaelmas daisy: afterthought; farewell

mignonette: "Your qualities surpass your charms."

milfoil: war

milkvetch: "You comfort me."

milkwort: hermitage

mimosa: sensitiveness

mint: virtue

mistletoe: "I surmount difficulties."

mock orange: counterfeit; memory

monkshood: chivalry; misanthropy

moonwort: forgetfulness

morning glory: affection; bond

moschatel: weakness

moss: maternal love

mosses: ennui

mossy saxifrage: affection

motherwort: concealed love

mountain ash: prudence

mouse-ear chickweed: ingenuous simplicity

mugwort: happiness

mulberry tree, black: "I shall not survive you."
mulberry tree, white: wisdom
mushroom: suspicion
mustard seed: indifference
myrobalan: privation
myrrh: gladness
myrtle: love

narcissus: egotism
nasturtium: patriotism
nemophila: "I forgive you."
nettle: slander; "You are cruel."
nettle tree: concert
night convolvulus: night
night-blooming cereus: transient beauty
nightshade: truth; silence

oak, white: independence
oak leaves: bravery
oak tree: hospitality
oats: the witching soul of music
oleander: "Beware."
olive tree: peace
orange blossom: chastity; bridal festivities
orange tree: generosity
orchid: thoughts
oregano: joy
osier: frankness
osmunda: dreams
ox eye: patience

palm: victory

pansy: (loving) thoughts

parsley: festivity

pasque flower: "You have no claims."

passion flower: faith

pea, everlasting: an appointed meeting; lasting pleasure

pea, sweet: departure; delicate pleasures

peach: "Your qualities, like your charms, are unequalled."

peach blossom: "I am your captive."

pear blossom: affection

pearly everlasting: never ceasing remembrance

pelargonium: eagerness

pennyroyal: "Flee away."

peony: shame; bashfulness

peppermint: warmth of feeling

periwinkle, blue: early friendship

periwinkle, white: pleasant memories

persimmon: "Bury me amid nature's beauties."

Peruvian heliotrope: devotion

petunia: "Your presence soothes me"; "Never despair."

phlox: unanimity; agreement

pimpernel: change

pine: pity

pine, pitch: philosophy

pink: boldness

pink, carnation: woman's love

pink, double Indian: always lovely

pink, double red: pure and ardent love

pink, mountain: aspiring
pink, single Indian: aversion
pink, single red: pure love
pink, variegated: refusal
pink, white: ingeniousness; talent
plane tree: genius
plum, Indian: privation
plum tree: fidelity
plum tree, wild: independence
polyanthus: pride of riches
polyanthus, crimson: the heart's mystery
polyanthus, lilac: confidence
pomegranate: foolishness
pomegranate flower: elegance
poplar, black: courage
poplar, white: time
poppy, oriental: silence
poppy, red: consolation
poppy, scarlet: extravagance
poppy, white: sleep
potato: benevolence
prickly pear: satire
primrose: youth; diffidence
primrose, evening: inconstancy
primrose, red: unpatronized merit
privet: prohibition
purple clover: provident
quaking grass: agitation

quince: temptation

ragged robin: wit

ranunculus: "You are radiant with charms and rich in attractions."

ranunculus, garden: "You are rich in attractions."

ranunculus, wild: ingratitude

raspberry: remorse

red catchfly: youthful love

red dianthus: lively and pure affection

red salvia: energy and esteem

reed, split: indiscretion

reeds, bundle of: music; amiability

rhododendrum, rosebay: danger; beware

rhubarb: advice

rocket: rivalry

rockrose (cistus): popular favor

rose: love

rose, Austrian: "Thou art all that is lovely."

rose, bridal: happy love

rose, burgundy: unconscious beauty

rose, cabbage: ambassador of love

rose, Carolina: "Love is dangerous."

rose, champion: "Only deserve my love."

rose, China: beauty always new

rose, Christmas: "Soothe my anxiety."

rose, daily: "Thy smile I aspire to."

rose, damask: brilliant complexion; freshness

rose, dog: pleasure and pain

rose, Guelder: winter; age

rose, hundred-leaved: pride; dignity of mind; grace

rose, Japan: "Beauty is your only attraction."

rose, La France: "Meet me by moonlight."

rose, maiden blush: "If you love me, you will find it out."

rose, multiflora: grace

rose, mundi: variety

rose, musk: capricious beauty

rose, musk (cluster): charming

rose, nephitos: infatuation

rose, red: bashful shame

rose, rock: popular favor

rose, single: simplicity

rose, thornless: early attachment

rose, unique: "Call me not beautiful."

rose, white: spiritual love; purity; "I am worthy of you."

rose, white (withered): transient impressions

rose, yellow: decrease of love; jealousy

rose, York and Lancaster: war

rosebay rhododendron: beware; danger

rosebud, moss: confession of love

rosebud, red: pure and lovely

rosebud, white: girlhood

rosemary: devotion; remembrance

roses, crown of: reward of virtue

roses (red and white together): unity

rudbeckia: justice

rue: disdain

rush: docility

_S_

rye grass (darnel): vice; changeable disposition

saffron: "Beware of excess."

saffron, crocus: mirth

saffron, meadow: "My happiest days are past."

sage: domestic virtue; esteem; good health

sainfoin: agitation

Saint John's wort: animosity; superstition

salvia, blue: thinking of you

salvia, red: energy and esteem; forever yours

saxifrage, mossy: affection

scabious: unfortunate love

scabious, sweet: widowhood

scarlet lychnis: sunbeaming eyes

scotch fir: elevation

sea thrift: sympathy

sensitive plant: sensibility; delicate feelings

shamrock: lightheartedness

shepherd's purse: "I offer you my all."

snapdragon: presumption

snowball: bound

snowdrop: hope

sorrel: affection

sorrel, wild: wit ill-timed

sorrel, wood: joy; maternal tenderness

southernwood: jest; bantering

Spanish jasmine: sensuality

spearmint: warmth of sentiment

speedwell: fidelity

speedwell, Germander: facility

speedwell, spiked: semblance

spiderwort: esteem not love

spindle tree: "Your charms are engraved on my heart."

spruce: hope in adversity; farewell

Star of Bethlehem: purity

starwort: afterthought

starwort, American: cheerfulness in old age; welcome to a stranger

stock: lasting beauty

stock, ten-week: promptness

stonecrop: tranquility

straw: agreement

straw, broken: quarrel; rupture of a contract

straw, whole: union

strawberry blossom: foresight

strawberry tree: esteem and love

sumac, Venice: splendor; intellectual excellence

sunflower, dwarf: adoration

sunflower, tall: haughtiness

swallowwort: cure for heartache

sweet basil: good wishes

sweet pea: delicate pleasures; departure

sweet sultan: felicity

sweet william: gallantry

sweetbrier, American: simplicity

sweetbrier, European: poetry; "I wound to heal."

sweetbrier, yellow: decrease of love

syringa: memory

syringa, Carolina: disappointment
tamarisk: crime
tansy, wild: "I declare war against you."
Teasel, Fuller's: misanthropy
thistle, common: austerity
thistle, Scotch: retaliation
thorn, apple: deceitful charms
thorns, branch of: severity
thrift: sympathy
thyme: courage; strength; activity
tree of life: old age
trefoil: revenge
trillium: modest beauty
truffle: surprise
tuberose: dangerous pleasures
tulip: fame
tulip, red: declaration of love
tulip, variegated: "You have beautiful eyes."
tulip, yellow: "I am hopelessly in love with you."
turnip: charity
valerian: an accommodating disposition
valerian, blue-flowered Greek: rupture
Venice sumac: intellectual excellence; splendor
Venus's-flytrap: deceit
Venus's-looking-glass: flattery
verbena: enchantment
verbena, pink: family union
verbena, scarlet: unite against evil; sensibility

verbena, white: guilelessness; "Pray for me."

veronica: fidelity

viburnum: thoughts of heaven

vine: intoxication

violet, blue: faithfulness; love; sweetness; loyalty

violet, dame: watchfulness

violet, sweet: modesty

violet, yellow: rural happiness

Virginian spiderwort: momentary happiness

virgin's bower: filial love

wake-robin: ardor

wallflower: fidelity in adversity

walnut: intellect; stratagem

water lily: purity of heart

watermelon: bulkiness

wax plant: susceptibility

wheat stalk: riches

white clover: good luck

white lily: purity; modesty

white mullein: good nature

white oak: independence

white pink: talent

white poplar: time

white rose, dried: "Death is preferable to loss of innocence."

whortleberry: treason

willow, creeping: love forsaken

willow, French: bravery and humanity

willow, water: freedom

willow, weeping: mourning

winter cherry (Chinese lantern plant): deception

wisteria: "Welcome, fair stranger"; "I cling to you."

witch hazel: a spell

wolfsbane: misanthropy

wood sorrel: joy; maternal tenderness

woodbine: fraternal love

wormwood: absence

xeranthemum: cheerfulness under adversity

yarrow: health; war

yew: sorrow

zinnia: thoughts of absent friends

Themes and Plants

Throughout history, human beings have attached special meanings to plants. Below is a list of themes, with a corresponding list of plants, culled from many cultures around the world, including the Victorian language of flowers. Use these thematic meanings to add additional significance to the personal significance that plants already hold for you.

THEME	PLANT
absence	wormwood
abundance	wheat
accommodation	heliotrope, valerian
activity	thyme
admiration	browallia
adoration	dwarf sunflower, safflower
advice	rhubarb
affection	cinquefoil, clematis, gillyflower, honeysuckle, jonquil, locust tree, morning glory, pear blossom, periwinkle, potentilla, red dianthus, saxifrage, sorrel
affluence	peony
afterlife	bay, daffodil, laurel, lily, myrrh
age	black mulberry, chrysanthemum, Guelder rose, myrtle, tree of life
agreement	phlox, straw
ambition	hollyhock, mountain laurel
amiability	bundle of reeds, jasmine

amusement	bladder nut tree
anticipation	gooseberry
ardor	arum, wake-robin
arts	acanthus
aspiration	mountain pink
assiduousness	ivy
audacity	larch
banter	southernwood
bashfulness	peony
beauty	amaryllis, apple tree, calla lily, citron, clematis, cowslip, French honeysuckle, gladiolus, hibiscus, jasmine, laburnum, lady slipper, lily, linden, magnolia, night-blooming cereus, orchid, parti-colored daisy, rose, stock, trillium, tulip, Venetian mallow, zinnia
beneficence	marsh mallow
benevolence	potato
betrothal	carnation
birth	birch, dittany of Crete, lotus, mistletoe, silver fir
bluntness	borage
boldness	larch, pink
bonds	convolvulus
bravery	French willow, oak leaves, thyme
bride	ivy geranium, jasmine, orange flower
brotherly love	azalea, gladiolus
calmness	buckbean
celibacy	bachelor's-button
change	fir, oak, pimpernel
character	gladiolus

charity	crocus, jonquil, turnip, wild grape
charm	gardenia, orchid, ranunculus, rose, zinnia
chasteness	acadia, lily, orange blossom, violet
cheerfulness	American starwort, Chinese chrysanthemum, coreopsis, crocus, jonquil, xeranthemum
chivalry	monkshood, yellow daffodil
Christmas joy	poinsettia
clarity	fennel
cleanliness	hyssop
comfort	lavender, milkvetch, pear tree, petunia, scarlet geranium
companionship	pond lily
compassion	allspice
confidence	hepatica, lilac polyanthus, liverwort
congeniality	geranium
consecration	frankincense
consolation	red poppy, snowdrop
constancy	bellflower, bluebell, canterbury bell, cedar, hyacinth, marigold, southernwood, tulip, violet
contemplation	chrysanthemum
contentment	camellia, chrysanthemum, houstonia
cordiality	peppermint
courage	aspen, pine, poplar, thyme
creation	lotus
cure	Balm of Gilead, cranberry, swallowwort
curiosity	sycamore
death	anemone, bay, black mulberry, cypress, elder, laurel, mistletoe, myrrh, parsley, poppy, weeping willow, yew
defender	iris

delicacy	centaury, cornflower, sensitive plant, sweet pea
desire	rose
devotion	azalea, cornflower, daffodil, heliotrope, lavender, rosemary, safflower
dignity	cloves, dahlia, dianthus, elm, hundred-leaved rose, ivy, magnolia, palm, pink
distinction	cardinal flower
divinity	cowslip, lily, lotus
docility	bulrush, rush
domesticity	flax, houseleek, sage
dreams	osmunda
durability	cornel tree, dogwood, oak
eagerness	pelargonium
early death	anemone
education	cherry blossom
elation	hazelnut
elegance	acacia (pink or white), dahlia, locust tree, pomegranate flower, yellow jasmine
eloquence	crape myrtle, lotus, water lily
enchantment	mandrake, verbena
encouragement	goldenrod
endurance	aspen, carnation, oak, pine, poplar
energy	chamomile, red salvia
ephemeral glory	hibiscus
esteem	red salvia, sage, spiderwort, strawberry tree
eternal life	chrysanthemum, evergreens, holly, seaweed
eternal love	evergreens, globe amaranth
eternity	apple tree, olive tree

everlasting love	evergreens
excellence	red camellia, strawberry
faith	passion flower, pine
faithfulness	hearts' ease, heliotrope, maple, violet, wild pansy
fame	apple blossom, tulip
family	geranium, ivy, pink verbena
farewell	Michaelmas daisy
fascination	fern, honesty
fate	flax, hemp
fecundity	hollyhock
feeling	peppermint
felicity	cornflower, jasmine, sweet sultan
femininity	linden
fertility	acorn, furze, gorse, gourd, hollyhock, mandrake, mistletoe, peony, wheat
festivity	parsley
fidelity	carnation, forget-me-not, ivy, lemon blossom, lilac, plum tree, rose, rosemary, speedwell, veronica, wallflower
finesse	sweet william
flexibility	bamboo, reed
foresight	holly, strawberry blossom
forgiveness	nemophila
frankness	osier
freedom	water willow
freshness	damask rose
friendship	acacia, arborvitae, blue periwinkle, forget-me-not, geranium, ivy, jasmine, plum
frivolity	bladder nut tree, London pride

frugality	chicory, endive
fruitfulness	grape, hollyhock
funeral	walnut tree
gaiety	brussel sprouts, butterfly orchis, primrose, yellow lily
gallantry	sweet william
generosity	gladiolus, heather, orange tree
genius	plane tree, sycamore
gentility	corn cockle
gentle-heartedness	raspberry
gentleness	lamb's-ears, magnolia, wisteria
girlhood	white rosebud
gladness	myrrh
glamor	dogwood
glory	bay, daphne, laurel
good fortune	artemis leaf, daffodil, garlic, heather, ivy, mint, myrtle, narcissus, oak, peach blossom, peony, sagebrush, verbena, wheat, white clover
good will	holly, poinsettia
good wishes	basil
good-naturedness	white mullein
goodness	mercury
grace	bamboo, birch, cowslip, jasmine, rose
grandeur	ash tree
gratitude	agrimony, campanula, canterbury bell, marigold
grief	aloe, harebell, marigold, weeping birch, weeping willow
guilelessness	white verbena
happiness	Cape jasmine, gardenia, johnny-jump-up, lily-of-the-valley, marjoram, mugwort, myrtle, rosemary, Virginian spiderwort,

	yellow violet
hardiness	clematis, pine, plum
health, healing	artemisia, cornflower, Iceland moss, ivy, mistletoe, myrrh, sage, yarrow
heavenly bliss	lily
heroism	oak
home	myrtle
honesty	honesty
honor	ivy, palm
hope	almond blossom, calla lily, forget-me-not, hawthorne, jasmine, petunia, plum, snowdrop, spruce
hospitality	oak tree
humility	bindweed, broom, convolvulus, hyssop, lilac, lily of the valley, morning glory, orchid, sweet woodruff, violet
imagination	lupine
immortality	acorn, balm, bay, calla lily, daphne, globe amaranth, ivy, lily, myrtle, peach, pine, sage
impatience	balsam, impatiens
incorruptibility	cedar of Lebanon
independence	white oak, wild plum tree
industry	bee orchis, flax, houseleek, red clover
ingenuity	geranium, pelargonium, white pink
innocence	alyssum, columbine, daisy, hyssop, lily, violet, white lilac
inspiration	angelica
intellect	Venice sumac, walnut
jest	southernwood
joy	burnet, Cape jasmine, crocus, gardenia, heart's ease, linden, marjoram, mugwort, oregano, parsley, wood sorrel

justice	coltsfoot, rudbeckia
kindness	raspberry
lamentation	aspen tree
levity	larkspur
liberty	live oak
life	acorn, ginseng
lightheartedness	shamrock
longevity	bamboo, chrysanthemum, fig, laurel, marigold, marjoram, mushroom, myrtle, oak tree, olive tree, orange blossom, peach blossom, plum, sage, sequoia
love	anemone, aspen, azalea, basil, basswood, betel nut, carnation, coreopsis Arkansa, daffodil, forget-me-not, furze, globe amaranth, gorse, heliotrope, honeysuckle, hyacinth, ivy, jasmine, lemon verbena, lime tree, linden, lotus flower, marjoram, moss, motherwort, myrtle, narcissus, peony, primrose, purple lilac, red catchfly, red chrysanthemum, rose, tulip, virgin's bower, woodbine, yellow acacia, yellow iris
loveliness	camellia, Indian pink, jasmine, lily, magnolia, orange blossom, rose, white hyacinth
loving thoughts	pansy
loyalty	violet
luster	crowfoot
luxury	chestnut tree
magnificence	magnolia
majesty	imperial lily, oak
marriage	betel nut, carnation, ivy, linden, myrtle, peony, rosemary
masculinity	peony
meditation	pansy

meekness	birch
melancholy	cypress
memory (-ies)	lavender, mock orange, syringa, white periwinkle
merit	cilantro, coriander, moss rose, red primrose
mildness	mallow
mirth	burnet, jonquil, larkspur, saffron crocus
modesty	hearts' ease, orchid, violet, white lily, wild pansy
mortality	pine
motherhood	cinquefoil, gourd, moss, wood sorrel
mourning	cypress, poppy, weeping birch, weeping willow, yew
music	bundle of reeds, oats
mystery	crimson polyanthus
neatness	broom
nobility	amaryllis, yellow crocus
optimism	chrysanthemum
passion	myrtle, white dittany of Crete
patience	chamomile, dock, fir tree, ox eye
patriotism	American elm, nasturtium
peace	lavender, lily, mistletoe, myrrh, myrtle, olive tree, verbana
peace of mind	hyacinth
perfection	orchid, pineapple, white lily
perseverance	canary grass, heather, laurel, southernwood, swamp magnolia, sycamore
persistence	canary grass, heather, laurel, southernwood, swamp magnolia, sycamore
philosophy	pitch pine
piety	wild geranium
play	hyacinth

pleasantness	white periwinkle
pleasure	grape, sweet pea
poetry	European sweetbrier
power	cress
preference	apple blossom, scented geranium
pride	amaryllis, gloxinia, hundred-leaved rose, polyanthus
prosperity	beech tree, evergreens, mandrake, mistletoe, peony
protection	agrimony, basil, cactus, cedar, evergreens, frankincense, garlic, holly, iris, ivy, juniper, mistletoe, mugwort, oak, rosemary, thistle
providence	purple clover
prudence	hyacinth, mountain ash
purification	frankincense, hyssop, myrrh
purity	lavender, lily of the valley, lotus, orange blossom, orchid, primrose, red rosebud, Star of Bethlehem, water lily, white lily
quick-sightedness	hawkweed
radiance	ranunculus
reason	goat's rue
rebirth	calla lily, elder tree, fennel, holly, ivy, lily of the valley, lotus, mistletoe, plum, pomegranate, sunflower, water lily, wheat, yew
recollection	periwinkle
reconciliation	filbert, hazel
refinement	dogwood, gardenia
regard	daffodil
regeneration	calla lily, elder tree, fennel, holly, ivy, lily of the valley, lotus, mistletoe, plum, pomegranate, sunflower, water lily, wheat, yew

relief	Christmas rose, Balm of Gilead
religiousness	passion flower
remembrance	American cudweed, everlasting, marigold, pansy, rosemary, strawflower, sunflower
repentance	rue
repose	blue convolvulus, buckbean
reserve	maple
resilience	bamboo, juniper, yew
rest	mistletoe, poppy
restfulness	myrtle
revery	flowering fern
riches	wheat stalk
rigor	lantana
sacrifice	oak
sadness	cypress, dead leaves
safety	traveller's joy
sculpture	hoya
sensibility	scarlet verbena
sensitivity	mimosa, sensitive plant
sensuality	Spanish jasmine
sentiment	spearmint
silence	belladona, nightshade, Oriental poppy
simplicity	American sweetbrier, lily, mouse-ear chickweed, single rose, wild rose
sincerity	chervil
sleep	white poppy
solace	evergreen thorn
solitude	heath, lichen

sorrow	lupine, purple hyacinth, weeping birch, weeping willow, yew
splendor	Venice sumac
sport	hyacinth
stability	beech, cress, ivy, mocassin, peony
stateliness	pecan
stoicism	boxwood
strength	bamboo, blackthorn tree, cedar, fennel, oak, pine, thyme
sturdiness	oak
success	coronilla, crown vetch, plum
succor	juniper
surprise	betony
sustenance	wheat
sweetness	honeysuckle, white lily
sympathy	balm, thrift
talent	white pink
taste	scarlet fuchsia
tears	helenium
temperance	azalea, lettuce
tenderness	wood sorrel
thankfulness	agrimony
thoughts	blue salvia, hearts' ease, johnny-jump-up, orchid, pansy, violet, zinnia
thriftiness	thyme
time	fir, white poplar
tranquility	broccoli, mudwort, stonecrop
transformation	frankincense
transience	morning glory, night-blooming cereus, withered white rose
triumph	bay, laurel, oak

truth	nightshade, white chrysanthemum
unanimity	phlox
understanding	oak
union	whole straw
unity	red and white roses together
utility	grass
versatility	spruce
victory	bay, ivy, laurel, palm, parsley, purple columbine
virginity	rue
virility	ginseng
virtue	magnolia, mint, oak, rose, rue, sage
vision	rue
vitality	sycamore
vivacity	houseleek
voluptuousness	cyclamen
voraciousness	lupine
warmth	cactus, peppermint, spearmint
wedding	ivy, ivy geranium, myrtle, orange flower
welcome	wisteria
wisdom	hazel nut, sage, sequoia, white mulberry tree
wit	cuckooflower, lychnis, ragged robin
worthiness	alyssum, cilantro, coriander, fennel, pink convolvulus
youth	apple tree, daisy, grape, magnolia, plum tree, primrose, sweet pea, white mulberry
zeal, zealousness	arum, elder
zest	lemon

Eric's garden took on a life of its own. My siblings purchased a tree in their nephew's memory. I was able to pick what I wanted and chose a white flowering crab apple. With the park bench I put there, it is a safe place to go to be "crabby" or just reflect and let emotions go. For the garden itself, I asked my other two children and Eric's girlfriend to pick out a meaningful perennial to plant. My daughter picked a butterfly bush, saying that maybe Eric would visit as a butterfly. My son chose Keys to Heaven, saying that maybe Eric could use the keys to help him get in. His girlfriend chose a baby blue scabosia (common name, pin cushion) because that was his favorite color. She also planted a miniature red rosebush reflecting their deep love. I find solace in making sure things are blooming and weed-free. Gardening is very therapeutic.

—Jayne Decker

GARDEN THEMES

A memory garden is special because it is personal. Using the language and symbolism of plants, you can make a personal, expressive statement to or about your loved one. Choosing a theme for your garden can help you clarify what it is you want to express and bring order to the design of your garden.

A garden theme develops and builds around a central idea. Let's say, for example, that your loved one enjoyed fine wines, perhaps even fancied himself or herself a connoisseur. You might erect an arbor in your garden, maybe with a chair or bench underneath, and plant grapevines that could grow up and envelope the canopy of the arbor. For years to come, the grape arbor would be a quiet place to sit with a glass of wine and remember ...

Many people never finish their memory gardens, letting it lead them in directions they never expected. Initially, though, it can be helpful to have a plan. In the following pages are some possible starting points—places to begin to focus and define your intentions.

You know your loved one better than anyone else. Let your imagination go. Find the design and plants that best celebrate your memories.

An Herb Garden of Memory

Well known for their healing properties, herbs are steeped in meaning and history. With rich scents, a variety of textures, and multiple uses, an herb garden evokes a deep engagement with nature through the senses. It can reflect a natural earthiness that perhaps was inherent in your loved one, or it can be planted in memory of your loved one who loved to cook. Here are several herbs to consider.

Germander is the herb of *joy.*

Mint speaks of *grief.*

Oregano speaks of *joy* and *happiness.*

Peppermint symbolizes *wisdom.*

Rosemary is the herb of *remembrance.*

Rue symbolizes *grief* and *understanding.*

Silver thyme symbolizes *remembering our happiness.*

Tansy means *life everlasting.*

Thyme reflects *courage.*

A Meditation Garden

A meditation garden reflects your contemplative loved one. Several appropriate plants are available.

Bee balm means *compassion* and *consolation*.

Canterbury bell is the flower of *gratitude*.

Daisy connotes *innocence* and *simplicity*.

Lamb's ear speaks of *healing*.

Lemon-scented geranium symbolizes *tranquility*.

Locust tree is the symbol of *natural change* and *"affection beyond the grave."*

Viburnum (snowball) represents *thoughts of heaven.*

White rose means *love* and *silence.*

The colors of these plants are significant. Purple is the color of spirit; blue is the color of peace; and white is the color of purity and silence. The green foliage reflects healing.

A meditation garden might be designed symmetrically to symbolize the importance of the balance a spiritual life moves toward. It has the feeling of solitude as the plants wrap around and enclose the sitting area. A statue of a religious figure of your choosing might sit in the center diamond as a focal point. An unobtrusive pebble path can lend tranquility.

A Garden in Remembrance of a Baby

Nothing evokes a more unspeakable sense of grief and helplessness than the loss of an infant. To create a garden in remembrance of a baby, you may want to choose plants that are delicate and light-colored to evoke the special softness that is a child. The garden might be formed or planted in the shape of a heart. Consider placing statues of angels, cherubs, or baby animals in the garden. Statues of maternal figures would also be appropriate. Any of the following plants can be used in remembrance of a child who has died. Trees are also popular choices, often planted at the gravesite or another meaningful setting.

Baby-blue-eyes

Baby's breath (*everlasting love*)

Baby's tears

Lamb's ear

Madonna lily

Moss (*maternal love*)

White daisies (*innocence and simplicity*)

White lilac (*youthful innocence*)

White miniature roses

A Patriotic Garden

You may want to create a patriotic memorial garden for a loved one who served in the armed forces or who simply had strong patriotic feelings. The obvious centerpiece for such a garden would be a flagpole displaying an American flag. The red, white, and blue of the American flag could be picked up in rows of red, white, and blue flowers.

If you wish to "paint" with flowers, be sure to plant them in masses of single colors; otherwise, the effect will be diluted. Annuals are your best bet, for they can provide brilliant color throughout the growing season. Dwarf varieties of **salvia**, which come in red, white, and blue, are one choice, but there are many other possibilities as well.

Nasturtium and **American elm** are two traditional symbols of *patriotism*. The **poppy** has long been used to honor soldiers killed on the battlefield. Other plants that might be appropriate for a soldier or patriot include the following.

Thyme (*courage*)

Bay (*glory*)

Laurel (*victory*)

Cedar (*strength*)

Oak (*bravery*)

A Spring Garden of Memory

As nature comes alive in the spring, a garden bursting forth with foliage and flowers can symbolize your loved one's rebirth into a different sphere. A spring bulb garden is relatively easy to plant and maintain, but it needs to be prepared in the fall. Below are some flowering bulbs and perennials with special significance.

Lily of the valley symbolizes a *return of happiness.*

Purple hyacinth speaks of *sorrow.*

Red tulip is a *declaration of love.*

Snowdrop is the emblem of *hope and consolation.*

Sprinkle seeds of **forget-me-nots** over the newly planted soil for additional meaning and a longer bloom period.

A Monet Garden for an Artist

One of the best known landscapes in the world, Claude Monet's garden at Giverny, can serve as a model for a memory garden for an artist, or anyone who loves and appreciates beauty. Monet's garden is known for its unconstrained growth and seasons of long bloom. Monet returned often to this subject. The flowers below are some of the plants found in the garden and in Monet's paintings.

Aster	Heavenly blue morning-glory
Blue salvia	Hollyhock
Clematis	Iris
Crocus	Nasturtium
Daffodil	Pearly gates morning glory
Dahlia	Peony
Daylily	Poppy
Delphinium	Rose
Dianthus	Sunflower

A Bird and Butterfly Garden

The best landscaping plan to attract birds and butterflies includes a variety of native plants. Evergreen trees such as the **spruce** provide escape cover for birds, winter shelter, and summer nesting sites; they also provide seeds from the pinecones. Birds will visit the spent flower heads of **echinacea (purple coneflower)** and **sunflowers**, grasping on to the swaying plant as they peck out the seeds. Tubular flowers, such as **bee balm**, are especially attractive to hummingbirds. Birds can be further encouraged to visit your garden with bird feeders, houses, and baths.

Butterflies like to light on the flat flower heads of plants such as **yarrow**, **coreopsis**, and **daisies**. Or, if you prefer, you can purchase butterfly houses at many garden centers. Much like birds, butterflies need protection from the wind, a place to lay their eggs, and water to drink. To attract monarch butterflies, plant **milkweed** in your garden.

Other bird and butterfly attracters include:

Aster	**Lavender**
Buddleia (butterfly bush)	**Lupine**
Butterfly weed	**Morning glory**
Cosmos	**Parsley**
Cotoneaster	**Petunia**
Crab apple	**Phlox**
Currant shrub	**Pincushion flower**
Delphinium	**Rosemary**
Dill	**Russian sage**
Fennel	**Shrubby cinquefoil**
Globe amaranth	**Thyme**
Honeysuckle	**Viburnum**
Horsemint	**Zinnia**

THE FRED BROMLEY
MEMORIAL GARDEN

Lil Bromley installed this memorial garden at the resort she and her husband, Fred, had frequented when he was alive. Lil used red in the garden to symbolize Fred's strength, love, courage, and passion; yellow for his wisdom and optimism; blue for their peaceful relationship; and orange for Fred's love of life and the joy he shared with others.

She similarly chose plants that expressed her feelings for her late husband and symbolized his life. Lil planted bright orange **nasturtium** to symbolize Fred's *patriotism*. Although nasturtiums must be replanted every spring, it is worth it for the splash of joyful orange blooms. (Nasturtiums grow well from seed.)

Lil selected seven perennials for the garden: **canterbury bells** and medium-blue **campanula** meaning *with gratitude*; red **chrysanthemums** representing *cheerfulness* and *rest* (the chrysanthemum is also the flower for November, Fred's birth month); bright yellow **coreopsis** for *cheerfulness*; **forget-me-nots** for *true love* and *promise of remembrance*; a **red rose** ("Veteran's Honor") meaning *I love you*; and an orange variety of **tiger lilies** signifying *enchantment*.

Two species of bulbs were planted in clumps of three to five— **yellow daffodils** symbolizing *great respect* and *regard*, and **red tulips** representing *a declaration of love*.

In addition, three herbs were planted: **oregano** to represent *joy* and *happiness*; **rosemary** meaning *remembrance* and *loyalty*; and **silver thyme** for *remembering our happiness*.

Two shrubs and a tree completed the plantings for Fred Bromley's memorial garden: two types of **butterfly bush**—"Royal Red" and "Empire Blue" (symbolizing *letting go*)—and a **spruce tree** for *farewell*.

To finish the design of the garden, Lil added a statue of a man and woman embracing, an angel statue, a river stone engraved with Fred's name, and stained-glass paving stones in a calla lily design. On the anniversary of her husband's death, Lil scattered his ashes on this site.

I just kept staring at that ugly piece of rocky ground to the left of my front door. It looked just the way I felt inside. I didn't know what the end result would be, but one hot day I just went out there with a pick and shovel. All my hurt and anger went into chopping up that miserable spot. Many weeks later I was standing there, knee-deep in an area about fifteen by twelve feet. I had finally removed all the rocks, leaving little dirt. It seemed to signal the end of my angry phase. It was time to bring in new, rich soil. Two years later, I have an amazing entry garden, the soil supporting a beautiful planting, brimming with life.

—Jill Olden

PREPARING, INSTALLING, AND
MAINTAINING YOUR GARDEN

*W*hile memorial gardens are special, created out of love, they still require labor to prepare, install, and maintain. Fortunately, the physical effort it takes to make a garden can often be a useful expenditure of energy. Sleep, for instance, is often negatively affected by grief. Sometimes when grieving, you need the physical release that a challenging project will take.

You may find comfort in inviting friends or family to help with the installation. Find people who are willing to listen and honor your feelings. Ask them to help you build your memorial garden so you can talk and reminisce as you commune with the healing forces of nature.

*Life
begins
the day
you start
a garden.*

Chinese
proverb

Preparation

STEP 1
Mark out the edges of your border. Typically irregular, curved edges blend best with landscapes. Use a garden hose to lay out the edges and curves to help you visualize the dimensions and shape of the garden.

STEP 2
Remove the sod, as well as all roots of anything currently growing in the space. (Watering well a day or two before will make this job easier.)

STEP 3
Till the soil to a depth of at least eight inches. Break up clods of soil and remove any rocks. Optional: If you have the time, at this point you may water, wait two weeks, and then remove any new growth. Turn over the soil again. This can eliminate a good portion of problematic weeds and grass in your garden.

STEP 4
Add generous quantities of the best compost you can find. All soil types benefit from adding quality compost. A four-inch layer is sufficient for average soils. If your soil is particularly poor, add several more inches.

STEP 5

Following the directions on the package, add a slow-release, complete organic fertilizer (i.e., one comprised of nitrogen, potassium, and phosphorous). Organic fertilizer is available at most garden centers.

STEP 6

Thoroughly mix the compost and fertilizer into the existing soil. Rake smooth.

THE WRIGLEY MEMORIAL GARDEN

*L*ocated on Catalina Island, the Wrigley Memorial Garden is dedicated to the memory of chewing gum magnate, William Wrigley Jr., who died in 1932. The garden began in 1935 as a collection of desert plants and was expanded in 1969 with an emphasis on plants that can be found naturally only on Catalina and other nearby California islands. Of particular concern to the foundation that manages the garden is the protection of rare and endangered species native to the island, including the Catalina Ironwood. Occupying nearly forty acres, the Wrigley Memorial Garden is a living legacy of Wrigley's love for the natural beauty of Catalina Island and his desire to preserve that beauty for future generations. The garden is open to visitors throughout the year.

Installation

STEP 7

Most nursery plants and seedlings can be planted in early spring, usually as soon as the soil can be worked in your area. Do not allow purchased plants to become overly dry before you plant them. Choose an overcast or cool day to plant. If that is not possible, plant in the early evening. Generally you should plant with the top of the potted soil even with the garden soil surface. If the plant roots are matted, slice the bound roots with a knife in several places or tease apart the root ball's surface.

If you are planting from seed, follow the directions on the seed packet. Some seeds should be planted in the fall; others can be started indoors in late winter or early spring, or planted directly into the ground in the spring when the ground temperature is sufficiently warm.

Note: Typically, plants have been hardened-off (acclimated to outdoor weather) by the nursery. If not, or if you are starting the plants indoors from seeds, you must take a few days to harden them. Begin by bringing them outside for several hours, gradually increasing the time until they are acclimated to outdoor conditions.

STEP 8

Water thoroughly. This is essential, even if the soil is moist. This step ensures that the roots are in contact with the soil.

STEP 9

Mulch, preferably with ground bark or bark chips. Mulching retains moisture, reduces weed growth, and greatly enhances your final project's appearance.

THE LINCOLN MEMORIAL GARDEN

*F*ounded in 1936 in Springfield, Illinois, as a living memorial to Abraham Lincoln, the Lincoln Memorial Garden contains native plants from the three Midwestern states in which Lincoln grew up—Kentucky, Indiana, and Illinois—and includes more than one hundred acres of rolling tree-covered hills, open meadows, and restored prairie. Landscape architect Jen Jensen's intent when he designed the garden was to recreate a sense of the Midwest as Lincoln himself might have experienced it. Species of trees growing in the garden include ash, basswood, beech, birch, buckeye, cherry, cottonwood, crab apple, cypress, dogwood, elm, fringe-tree, gum, hackberry, hickory, hop hornbeam, linden, magnolia, maple, mulberry, oak, osage orange, persimmon, plum, redbud, redhaw, sassafras, service berry, silverbell, thorn, tulip tree, walnut, willow, and yellowwood. The garden, which is open to the public year round, is designed around a series of intersecting paths that have as their nodes a number of "council rings"—stone benches arranged in a circle where visitors can gather. In 1992 the Lincoln Memorial Garden was placed on the National Register of Historic Places.

Maintenance

Your garden will need more water as the plants establish their root systems and adjust to their new home, particularly during the first season. Keep the soil moist, not wet, in the beginning, gradually decreasing your watering schedule. The following season, water as indicated for your climate, always watering deeply to encourage deep root growth, which makes for hardier plants.

Removing spent blooms (deadheading) prevents seed formation. The plants use that energy for increased vigor and often another round of blooms.

Plant disease is best approached by prevention. Healthy plants are much less susceptible to pests or disease. Purchase only plants with healthy foliage. Maintain an appropriate watering schedule. Keep weeds at bay. Make sure your plants have nutrients by fertilizing them regularly. Do what you can to attract birds to your yard to dine on garden pests. If these measures are not sufficient, natural, organic products that address plant infestations are available at your local nursery.

After the growing season and your plants have gone dormant, remove the dead foliage to reduce disease carryover to the next season. Also, mulch the bed with leaves, wood chips, peat moss, or other types of organic mulch to retain moisture and reduce plant damage from temperature fluctuations.

Before each subsequent growing season, top-dress your garden's soil with two to three inches of quality compost or add an organic fertilizer to ensure your plants have the nutrients they need for another season.

Each state has extension offices that offer a wealth of information about local horticulture concerns. They can answer questions about your region's typical soil, plant diseases, the local gardening zone, the first and last frost dates for your area, and many other topics.

THE EWING AND MURIEL KAUFFMAN MEMORIAL GARDEN

The Ewing and Muriel Kauffman Memorial Garden occupies two acres within the Kauffman Legacy Park in Kansas City, Missouri. The garden is a posthumous gift to the people of Kansas City from a couple whose influence in the community was unrivaled during their lifetimes. Open to the public year round, the garden contains more than 300 varieties of plants, including vintage and modern perennials, annuals, shrubs, bulbs, and trees. The garden is divided into three main areas: the Green Garden, the Secret Garden, and the Parterre Garden, all of which are designed with water displays. Annual displays are changed at least three times a year. Blue spruce and maples have been planted to honor Muriel Kauffman's Canadian heritage. Brick pathways link several pavilions and arbors, inside of which visitors can find refuge from the warm Missouri summer sun. A conservatory containing six large palm trees and other plants also provides shelter for visitors.

When my husband died suddenly ten years ago, the shock and grief were overwhelming. It was all I could do to get through each day, and I could not bear to think of the future. I had a large, beautiful perennial garden, so there was always gardening work to be done. Gradually, without even realizing it, I began making plans to rearrange some plants and add new ones. Gardening was the first area of my life where I could look toward the future.

—Joyce W.

Our son Mark was born with Smith Lempri Obitz syndrome, an extremely rare condition. In fact, Mark was only the fourteenth case ever to be diagnosed. While the average life expectancy for children with the syndrome is only four years, Mark lived until his twenty-second birthday. After he died, we decided to start what we now refer to as "Markie's bed." One dear friend bought a birdbath, which is in the center of the bed. Friends donated lots of perennials, which made us realize how much he was truly loved. Little by little what started as a small bed is still growing. We added some birdhouses, and it's so peaceful to watch new baby birds learning to fly and to know that life does go on. The joy of watching all the butterflies, bumblebees, and hummingbirds always makes us realize that Markie is much happier now and that for once he can run and play just like other little boys. Each year on his birthday we buy a new garden statue to remind us of someone special who added so much to so many lives. Each time we enter Markie's garden we are reminded of Markie and all the other wonderful people God has sent into our lives.

—Jan Weber

ACCESSORIES FOR A MEMORY GARDEN

*A*ccessories such as benches, chairs, arbors, trellises, statuary, birdhouses, birdbaths, bird feeders, paths, walkways, plaques, engraved stones, and artificial lighting can provide a finishing touch to your memory garden project. Carefully chosen accessories can turn an ordinary garden into a truly special one. Whether the purpose is functional or purely ornamental, accessories can enhance the inspirational quality of your memory garden. Use your personal taste and preferences to add depth and texture to your garden.

A garden is a friend you can visit anytime.

Unknown

Garden Furniture

A place to sit is essential in a garden of tribute. You need a place where you can stop, sit, and let your concerns melt away. What better way to connect with the spirit and memory of your loved one and touch the warmth within your own heart than by sitting in a beautiful spot of nature created in love? Whether you take a cup of tea, a book, or just your thoughts with you to the garden, you will want a place to rest comfortably in the serenity of this special place.

Garden furniture need not be grand, ornate, or expensive. Different regions of the country feature different materials and bench styles. In the Rocky Mountains, sandstone is popular. New England gardens commonly have Adirondack-style benches and chairs. Battery-style park benches are easy to find and affordable. Rustic styling has become more popular over the years, and garden centers are beginning to carry more of this unique outdoor furniture. Classic lines in traditional teak or cedar are handsome in any landscape and are weather-resistant. The Monet garden bench has an arched ladder-back design. Weatherized wicker is comfortable and inviting. Cast iron furniture is durable and easy to maintain.

Wooden furniture needs to be maintained with regular applications of a quality wood sealer. Even naturally weather-resistant woods such as teak, cedar, or redwood benefit from periodic sealing. Depending on the extremes of your particular climate and the type of garden furniture you choose, you may need to protect or shelter your furniture during the winter.

Within the appropriate place, a garden swing is a great alternative to a garden bench. If it fits into your landscape, a tree swing or a freestanding unit recalls a simpler way of life. Gentle rocking provides a relaxing vantage from which to view your garden.

Many garden benches and swings can be personalized with an engraved inscription on a small brass plaque.

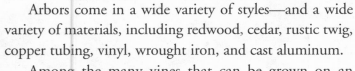

Arbors and Trellises

Memory gardens are refuges. An arbor at the entry to a memory garden can set it off from the rest of your property, creating privacy and sanctuary. Nestling within an arbor planted with morning glories or heavenly-scented climbing roses can give you moments of sweet repose for remembering the gift of your loved one. In addition to providing an entry gate or alcove for seating, arbors also provide shelter from the sun on hot summer days.

Arbors come in a wide variety of styles—and a wide variety of materials, including redwood, cedar, rustic twig, copper tubing, vinyl, wrought iron, and cast aluminum.

Among the many vines that can be grown on an arbor, **grapes** and **climbing roses** are long-standing favorites. In very warm climates, **bougainvillea** provides stunning color. For cooler zones, the versatile **clematis** is a good choice. **Passionflower**, which is traditionally associated with Christian faith, is a symbolically appropriate vine for a memory garden. **Honeysuckle**, with its unmistakable fragrance, pleases both the eye and the nose. Other possibilities include **silver lace vine**, **trumpet vine**, and **Virginia creeper**, or **woodbine**.

If you don't have room for an arbor, you may want to consider a decorative trellis. Like arbors, trellises provide support for climbing vines, and, like arbors, they come in many different shapes, sizes, and materials.

Statuary

Statuary is another accessory that can enhance your garden. Whatever type of object you choose—traditional or contemporary, sophisticated or rustic, serious or lighthearted—all that matters is that it speaks to you.

Religious figures are obvious choices for a memory garden, reinforcing, as they do, the garden's spirit and purpose. Some figures you might select include St. Francis of Assisi, the patron saint of nature; St. Fiacre, the patron saint of gardeners; Kuan Yin, the compassionate Buddha; Jesus' Mother Mary, another symbol of compassion; angels and cherubs; or Shiva, the Hindu god, destroyer of illusion. Animal figures with specifically Christian implications include the fish (Christ), the pelican (redemption), and the dove (God's promise to man and Christ's resurrection),

For a more whimsical touch, consider fantastic subjects such as garden sprites and fairies. Statues of animals can add a "natural" touch to the garden. Below are some common animal subjects and their symbolic meanings. For more personal meaning, consider a statue that resembles your loved one's favorite pet.

Bluebird—*happiness*	**Dog**—*loyalty*	**Dove**—*peace*
Elephant—*sagacity*	**Fish**—*good luck*	**Lamb**—*innocence*
Lark—*joy*	**Lion**—*courage*	**Owl**—*wisdom*
Rabbit—*resourcefulness*	**Swan**—*purity*	**Turtle**—*endurance*

Birdbaths, Houses, and Feeders

A vast array of birdbaths, houses, and feeders are available if you would like to indulge in the pleasures of birdwatching. In addition to attracting birds, birdbaths, houses, and feeders can add delightful decorative elements to a garden.

The proper combination of quality materials and good design makes an effective birdhouse. If you have specific species of birds you want to attract, go to a birding center to be certain the home you purchase will invite the species you want.

Birdbaths and feeders should be placed where predators, particularly domesticated cats, and food thieves, particularly squirrels, can't get to them easily.

Seed-eating birds are the most common visitors to the backyard. Sunflower seeds are a favored food for a number of desirable species and are considered by many to be the most effective way to attract the greatest number of birds. In the wintertime, suet feeders will attract woodpeckers, nuthatches, finches, and other species. To attract hummingbirds, hang one or more feeders that dispense sweet nectar. Be sure to clean the feeders and change the liquid frequently.

For suggestions on creating a bird and butterfly garden, see pages 64–65.

What I did was set up bird feeders because Eddie so loved his birds. I remember on the morning of his death—it was just daybreak—and as they carried his body to the ambulance, the birds were singing everywhere! Everyone noticed. It seemed the birds sensed something was very different and were saying goodbye (or maybe hello) to him.

—DeeAnn Burnette-Lundquist

Paths and Walkways

Many garden designs have a walkway leading to a sitting area. Both the walkway and the area in front of the bench need to be paved with stepping stones, pebbles, or other material to prevent the ground from becoming muddy. Ordinary bricks can be used as well, as can any preformed paving stone from a home supply center. Garden centers can usually direct you to a stone yard that sells flagstone-type paving materials, as each area of the country has a stone indigenous to its geology. Stepping stones can also be made from large logs sliced in pieces three to four inches thick and then treated with a wood preservative. Some artisans make stepping-stones from stained glass in an array of beautiful designs, which are then weather-treated and preserved with a sealant. For the do-it-yourselfer, forms are available to make your own cobblestone-type path from concrete, allowing you to mix the cement yourself and add a colorant of your liking. To soften the look of the path, plant grass or a low ground cover between the pavers. Low-growing varieties of thyme are especially suited for this type of planting.

Plaques and Engraved Stones

A garden of tribute is intensely personal, a place to express what is in your heart. Plaques and engraved stones are one more way to add rich meaning to the space. Favorite inscriptions, original poetry, birth dates, inspirational quotes, prayers, and, of course, your loved one's name are all examples of things you can have engraved on a stone or plaque. Stone yards can help you find a stonecutter in your area. Every area has local artists who work with different materials. If you choose a wooden plaque, be sure to seal it with a quality wood preservative.

Whether you hang the engraving on a wall, nail it to the trunk of a tree, or nestle it in a border at the edge of the garden, adding an inscription is a wonderful way to declare the intent of your garden.

Lighting

Lighting can also be used to impact the ambiance of outdoor areas. A lit garden increases the amount of time comfortably available to you. Illuminating paths, statuary, and other garden features brings a different dimension to the garden at night. Casting a light upwards on a special tree or shrub creates a feeling of expansive peacefulness. Garden torches are charming lighting features that do not involve electricity.

One way to personalize your memory garden is to incorporate your loved one's zodiac sign into the design.

Aries	ram	March 21–April 19
Taurus	bull	April 20–May 20
Gemini	twins	May 21–June 20
Cancer	crab	June 21–July 22
Leo	lion	July 23–August 22
Virgo	virgin	August 23–September 23
Libra	scales	September 24–October 23
Scorpio	scorpion	October 24–November 21
Sagittarius	archer	November 22–December 21
Capricorn	goat	December 22–January 19
Aquarius	water bearer	January 20–February 18
Pisces	fish	February 19–March 20

Other Options

From the serious to the whimsical, from the antique to the modern, the array of garden accessories is vast. You can buy a surprising range of sundials, wind chimes, copper or brass art, obelisks, and gazing balls. A browse through one of the many garden supply catalogs, a stroll through a good-sized garden center, or time spent on the Internet will inspire you to complete and complement your garden of memory in your own unique way.

Another option for personalizing your garden is to use colors or objects that reflect your loved one's birthstone.

Month	Birthstone
January	garnet
February	amethyst
March	aquamarine or bloodstone
April	diamond
May	emerald
June	pearl
July	ruby
August	peridot or sardonyx
September	sapphire
October	opal
November	topaz
December	turquoise

Our son was murdered almost eleven years ago. The authorities believed it would be impossible to find his body. We have never had a funeral or memorial service. A garden was a way to memorialize our son and cope with the sorrow.

I can't tell you how much this whole process has meant, and still means, to us. Just about every evening my husband and I sit out beside the garden when it is shady. We watch the plants, the birds at the bird feeder and birdbath. We frequently see a male cardinal, which has come to be my symbol for Tim. I always thought that cardinals just made a small "cheep-cheep" sound, but the day we completed the initial planting, a cardinal flew to the branch of a tree right above the garden and sang and sang and sang! Now I frequently hear not only the cheep-cheep sound but also this more melodious singing, which I don't have the words to describe.

—Penny P. Moreau

6

DEDICATING YOUR GARDEN

*T*hroughout history, every culture and every religion has acknowledged death with some sort of ritual or ceremony. The ritual, whether holding a funeral, sitting Shiva, or scattering ashes, orients the survivors in the midst of their grief and is an important step in the healing process.

The installation of your garden might be completed with a ceremony dedicating this space to your loved one's memory. Creating the garden directs the energy of your grief toward healing. Engaging in a completion ritual is another big step along the path. With gardening complete, a dedication ritual brings your intention into sharper focus. You have invested yourself in this process of creation for a reason. This garden celebrates the life and love you shared. It honors what has past, a tangible, visible reflection of a life that was lived and will be remembered. The

*One is
nearer
God's Heart
in a garden
Than
anywhere
else on
earth.*

Dorothy
Frances
Gurney

ceremony also acknowledges the spirit inherent in life, inherent in the natural world—life always changing, always moving forward, always evolving from one level of awareness to the next. It is change that we resist.

Extend much compassion toward yourself when preparing to dedicate your garden. Rituals are powerful. The dedication is a step to be taken with consciousness. The most meaningful ceremonies are individualized to reflect the life being honored and the lives touched by the loss. Therefore, the following suggestions are offered only as starting points. Spend time contemplating and discussing what you and others involved want to incorporate into this time. Reflect on the gifts you received from this person. In what ways are you a better person for having had him or her in your life?

It may help to remember your life with your loved one in a linear fashion. What were the treasures uncovered along your blessed journey with this soul? Elevate your mind to the highest point of view possible and see the learning you engaged in together. See the places in your heart touched by this person that no one else has ever touched. Through the memories and the sorrow, see if you can find the sweet gratitude for what you shared and for the place your soul has now brought you. Contemplate, from the highest mind and heart, what this grief has taught you. Consciously choose what you will hold as most important from this experience. Release any remaining residue of guilt and resentment, of judgment toward yourself, your departed, or anyone else. Vow to come through this to a place of increased awareness of the purity and perfection of life in all its raw, stinging forms.

When you are ready, open your heart and dedicate this spot of heaven on earth in the spirit of highest truth, utmost beauty, deepest integrity, and unconditional love.

REMEMBRANCE RITUALS

- Set aside a specific time for the ritual. If you like, invite others to be present.
- Ask for spiritual support at the ceremony.
- Incorporate the natural ceremonial elements of fire and water.
- Display favorite pictures.
- Reflect on and share favorite memories.
- Share what you will miss.
- Talk about something you learned from this special person.
- Read poems that speak meaningfully to you, or write your own for the service.
- Incorporate spiritual readings that are meaningful to you.
- Write, and read, a letter to your loved one.
- State your intentions for the garden. Say whatever feels right to you.
- Use this time to place an engraved stone or statuary in the garden.
- Scatter your loved one's ashes in the garden, if that is what you have chosen.
- In future years, share seeds or plant slips from this special garden.

When Penny Moreau and her family dedicated Tim's garden (see pp. 92-93), Penny read aloud "Tomorrow There Will Be Flowers" by Dan Gill (reprinted on the opposite page). You may find these words comforting as you create a ritual for your own memory garden. You may also find beauty and solace in the poem "Memorial Day" by Mary Logue, which is reprinted on pages 100-101.

Tomorrow There Will Be Flowers

Dan Gill

There is solace in the garden. For grief or disappointment, the garden provides a place of refuge and healing. People are often moved to plant a garden upon the loss of someone they love. Gardening is an act of creation—an affirmation of life continuing on despite what has happened.

I think the human spirit is most fulfilled when we create and nurture. Gardeners somehow understand that gardening is so much more than growing plants. It fills a deep yearning for the connection we need to something beyond ourselves. A gardener comprehends the life in plants and their quiet struggle to live. I believe this connection to green life can be part of what sustains us in time of emotional stress.

I have heard gardening called a pastime or hobby. But gardeners know the truth. Gardening is a partnership between the plants and the gardener to the benefit of both. We often focus on what we do for our gardens, but stop and think of what you receive in return. Go out into the garden and touch a leaf or smell a flower. You will feel the life-giving power that waits only for you to notice it, and it will fill your heart with what you need most.

Gardening is nothing if not a belief in tomorrow—that seeds sown today will germinate and grow, and in their own time the plants will bloom to brighten our lives. Sometimes the belief that tomorrow will come is so important. And even more important is the desire to be there and see what life has to unfold—to know that no matter how terrible things are now, tomorrow there will be flowers.

Memorial Day

by Mary Logue

I

Three days of shrouded sky.
Below it we open up the ground
and stick flowers in
a pattern which is pleasing
to the eye when seen from above.

Bending and rising, we finally worship
what we ought: the land, the rising warmth,
the spirit that runs in us like sap,
the energy that makes life fill out
the fans of a day lily.

II

Two crab apple trees
in such full bloom the eye wearies
of tracing the petals that lace the
fretwork of branches. I try to
imagine a person suddenly budding
from ever pore—such great beauty!
We would declare hosanna.

III

One year ago today
we gathered on the back lawn:
our family, three daughters and a tired
father. His body thinned to awkward grace,
hands floated to carry a cigarette to his lips.
We all knew it would not happen again.
The dogs chased each other on the grass
and his eyes flew after them.

IV

No parents left, we plant flowers
and water trees, we lift an eye
to empty sky, a freighted gray,
we give the day away, a waft
of lilac scent, a handful of
petals lent, and remember
what a time we've had.

My beautiful eighteen-year-old daughter—a lover of flowers, of gardens, of beauty—died in a car crash two years ago. On her first birthday after her death, I took sunflower seeds to several people special to her. She had been known for her love of sunflowers and for being a sunny person. This year on her birthday I planted a Japanese magnolia for her because she always laughed at me for being repeatedly overjoyed at the first magnolia blooms down the street from our home.

—Nancy Lockett

I have a beautiful perennial garden that began in a very small space at a time when I was so overcome with grief I didn't know how I would be able to go on. I knew only that I had to dig in the dirt. It really wasn't conscious; it was more a pull. I would simply sit on the ground and work the dirt. That was five years ago, and my garden now fills my side yard and part of my backyard. Undoubtedly it was (and definitely continues to be) my medicine. I think the gardening helped on a completely different level, bypassing the mind and even the emotions, going straight to the soul. I can't begin to articulate the level of comfort and, eventually, healing it brought me, and the balance and harmony it continues to bring.

—DeeAnn Burnette-Lundquist

FINAL THOUGHTS

*W*hen my brother died a number of years ago, the question arose how best to memorialize him. Because he was an avid gardener and his death took place at a hospice, we chose to donate money to the hospice for a garden that would reflect the person he was. We felt this would be a gift to future residents, as well as to visitors and staff.

It wasn't until after we made this decision that I came to understand why David had spent so much time outside, digging and planting in the dirt. I discovered that when I spent time outside I felt tuned into all of creation—the expansive sky, the movement of air, the sounds of birds, the activity going on within the soil. These all pointed to a much larger picture. I began to find understanding in the cycles of the seasons—birth, death,

Cry
if you
must,
but
plant
if you
can.

Kay
Frey

dormancy, and renewal. I came to see that I was powerless to control the forces of nature, whether it was a strong wind blowing over tender young stalks or a deer grazing on my long-awaited blooms.

I found peace in accepting the inevitability of natural occurrences. Experiencing nature in a deeply intimate way transformed my life as the connections made outside integrated within.

Through my professional and personal experience, I have learned that unresolved grief—be it from a recent loss or one more distant—leaves a residue in our being, and each subsequent loss taps into that unresolved grief. It can result in a numbing effect, a lingering anger or sadness, but the result is the same. Our true essence becomes clouded.

My wish for you is that you know healing from the pain of loss, that you know the peace of acceptance that transcends all circumstances. And that you know that as your loved one graced and blessed your life, you have graced them and blessed this earth with a healing garden made with love.

When I see the balsam bloom or the quince or almond bushes flower, I will always think of my dad. When I see the violets in the spring or the scillia and the johnny-jump-ups, I think of my grandfather. These flowers and bushes help me keep a connection to them. I also love to share my garden with others, so my garden has a connection with the people I love. It is comforting for me, and when I walk in a friend's yard and see my grandfather's violets or my dad's balsam, I know my loved ones live on.

—Jeanne Norton

This past spring, some friends and I held a garden tour in our town in my daughter's memory and raised money for the memorial scholarship, which the school had started. None of us had any experience in this, but it was a glorious day. Everything was perfect except the reason we were having it. It was a day of beauty for the community. A wholesaler donated plants to sell, so I feel all those plants now beautifying our town are another part of her legacy.

—Nancy Lockett

And that is what this is all about:
honoring the legacy of these beautiful souls who have graced our lives.

SELECTED PLANTS
ARRANGED BY COMMON NAME

The following plants have been selected for their special significance for memorializing a loved one. This list is in no way intended to be comprehensive. It is merely offered as a starting point as you consider what sort of living tribute is most appropriate for your particular situation.

There are countless species, varieties, and cultivars of plants for you to choose from. To locate those that are best suited for the region in which you live, visit local garden centers and nurseries. Some plants have a soil pH preference—which is to say that they prefer soil that is either alkaline or acid. To determine the type of soil you have in your garden, contact your local county extension office. For specific planting and gardening information, there are many excellent gardening publications and resources available.

Common Name	*Botanical Name*	Type	Zone	Light
acacia	*Acacia*	evergreen shrub or tree	7-10	full sun
aloe	*Aloe*	succulent	9-10	full sun to partial shade
anemone (windflower)	*Anemone*	flowering bulb or perennial	6-10	full sun to partial shade
artemisia (tarragon)	*Artemisia*	perennial shrub or herb	3-10	full sun
aster, hardy (Michaelmas daisy)	*Aster*	perennial	4-9	full sun
baby's breath	*Gypsophila*	perennial or annual	3-9	full sun

Comments

The acacia symbolized birth and death for the ancient Egyptians. In Europe, it symbolizes immortality. There are many types, all of which produce tiny yellow flowers.

Aloe symbolized grief in the Victorian language of flowers. It can be grown as a houseplant in northern zones if taken outdoors in the summer and kept in a well-lighted, dry place in the winter. Produces flowers in the spring.

The name "anemone" is derived from the Greek word for wind, and the flower is also known as the "windflower." The anemone evokes the transitoriness of life and traditionally symbolizes an early death. It is associated with the death of Adonis in ancient Greek mythology and with the blood of saints in Christianity. In Chinese folklore, anemones are planted over graves. Colors include white, mauve, lavender, pink, crimson, blue, rose, and scarlet.

In classical mythology, artemisia was sacred to Artemis (Diana) and believed to have healing qualities. Artemisia is valued for its aromatic gray-green or silver foliage. Also known as tarragon, wormwood, southernwood, or dusty miller.

Asters are a large and diverse group of plants with masses of daisy-like flowers. Most varieties bloom from late summer into fall. Flowers are white, blue, red, pink, or lavender with yellow centers. Good for cut flowers. Also called Michaelmas daisy.

Baby's breath is a summer bloomer, producing tiny, airy white or pink blossoms in large clusters. An excellent cut or dried flower.

Common Name	*Botanical Name*	Type	Zone	Light
balm (lemon balm)	*Melissa officinalis*	annual herb	all	full sun or partial shade
bamboo	several genera	evergreen shrub	7-10	full sun
basil, sweet or ornamental	*Ocimum basilicum*	annual herb	all	full sun
bee balm (bergamot)	*Monarda didyma*	perennial	4-9	full sun to partial shade
birch	*Betula*	deciduous tree	2-4	full sun
brunnera	*Brunnera*	perennial	4-5	partial shade
butterfly bush (buddleia)	*Buddleia*	deciduous shrub	5-10	full sun

Comments

Balm, or lemon balm, is a traditional symbol for immortality. It signifies sympathy in the Victorian language of flowers and was often used in memorials. Produces small white or yellow flowers in late summer and early fall that are very attractive to bees.

In China, bamboo symbolizes resiliency in the face of adversity. These members of the grass family have slender, arching stems and feathery foliage. Most grow rapidly.

Because basil is the most sacred of all plants to Hindus, it is planted on Hindu graves, and each believer is buried with a basil leaf. Its aromatic leaves repel mosquitoes. Tiny white or purplish flowers appear in late summer.

Bee balm, or bergamot, grows in bushy clumps, 2 to 4 feet tall, 2 to 3 feet wide. Clusters of pink, red, or lavender flowers are much loved by hummingbirds and bees.

In Celtic folklore, the birch represented the birth of new life. The weeping birch, like the weeping willow, is a symbol of grief. Foliage turns yellow in the fall.

Brunnera produces blue star-like flowers in mid to late spring. The early appearance of blooms make brunnera a good companion for spring-flowering bulbs. Also called Siberian forget-me-not and Siberian bugloss.

Butterfly bush, or buddleia, is fast-growing and hardy. Varieties range from 4 to 15 feet in height. White, purple, red, pink, lilac, or blue flowers appear in early to late summer.

Common Name	Botanical Name	Type	Zone	Light
calendula (pot marigold)	*Calendula officinalis*	annual	all	full sun, but cool temperatures
campanula (bellflower)	*Campanula*	biennial or perennial	3-10	full sun to partial shade
centaurea (cornflower)	*Centaurea*	perennial or annual	4-10	full sun
chrysanthemum	*Chrysanthemum*	perennial	4-10	full sun
coreopsis (tickseed)	*Coreopsis*	perennial	3-9	full sun
cotoneaster	*Cotoneaster*	deciduous or evergreen shrub	2-8	full sun or partial shade

Calendula, or pot marigold, grows 1 to 2 feet tall and blooms throughout the summer. Flowers are orange, yellow, or cream. A good cut flower.

Campanula, also known as bellflower, canterbury bell, or harebell, produces flowers that are blue, purple, pink, or white. Its sturdy erect stems help make it an excellent cut flower. Smaller varieties are good choices for rock gardens.

The cornflower was a popular flower among the ancient Egyptians who often used it in funeral tributes for the dead. It is traditionally associated with healing. Perennial varieties are generally referred to as centaurea. Annual varieties are commonly called cornflower, bachelor's-button, dusty miller, or sweet-sultan. All make good cut flowers.

Known in parts of southern Europe as "Fiori dei Morte" (the flower of death), the chrysanthemum was traditionally offered to the dead on All Saints Day. A symbol of eternal life, it is closely associated with funerals. Flowers are white, red, pink, orange, yellow, purple, lavender, or russet.

Coreopsis, or tickseed, is a hardy perennial that produces bright yellow, daisy-like flowers throughout the summer into fall. It is adaptable to most soil types and easy to grow, with a tendency to self-sow. Great as a cut flower.

There are many forms of cotoneaster, from low-growing mats to small trees. White, pink, or violet blooms appear in spring, followed by red or black berries.

Common Name	Botanical Name	Type	Zone	Light
crab apple, flowering	Malus	deciduous tree	3-8	full sun
crape myrtle	Lagerstroemia	deciduous shrub	7-10	full sun
currant, flowering	Ribes Saxifragaceae	deciduous shrub	2-10	full sun to partial shade
cypress	Cypressus	conifer tree	7-8	full sun
daffodil (narcissus)	Narcissus	blooming bulb	3-9	full sun to partial shade

Comments

Red, white, or pink blooms appear on the flowering crab apple tree in early spring. Many varieties are quite fragrant, and most produce small fruit that attracts birds.

Crape myrtle produces pink, white, red, or lavender blooms from July to September. It needs a moist, rich, well-drained soil, and grows to heights of 6 to 30 feet.

The flowers of the currant are generally yellow or chartreuse, but some varieties produce red flowers. Spring blooms are followed by edible summer berries.

Associated with Pluto, the god of the underworld in classical mythology, the cypress became a symbol of immortality because it was believed to have the power to preserve bodies. The cypress signified death and mourning in the Victorian language of flowers, and is also associated with death in Chinese lore. It is often planted in cemeteries. The cypress tree tends to have a narrow, upright profile, and can exceed 100 feet in height.

In Greek mythology, Narcissus was a young man who became infatuated with his own reflection in a pool of water. He died from his self-obsession and was transformed into a flower. The ancient Greeks believed that the narcissus, or daffodil, thrived in Hades, hence its long association with death and burial. The Egyptians associated the daffodil with the underworld as well, using the flower in funeral wreaths, and this association reappears in the Victorian language of flowers. Like other spring-blooming bulbs, the daffodil is a symbol of hope and rebirth. The yellow, white, cream, pink, apricot, orange, or red flowers are excellent for cutting.

Common Name	Botanical Name	Type	Zone	Light
daphne	Daphne	deciduous, semi-evergreen, or evergreen shrub	5-9	full sun to partial shade
daylily	Hemerocallis	perennial	3-10	full sun to partial shade
delphinium	Delphinium	perennial	3-8	full sun, but not too hot and dry
dianthus (carnation, pink, maiden pink, sweet william)	Dianthus	evergreen perennial or annual	3-7	full sun
dogwood, flowering	Comus	deciduous tree	5-10	full sun to partial shade
fennel	Foeniculum vulgare	annual herb	all	full sun

Comments

The daphne symbolized immortality in the Victorian language of flowers. Clusters of small, often fragrant lilac-like flowers appear in spring or early summer, and fruit ripens in the fall. Excellent for rock gardens, borders, or as a specimen plant, but be aware that the fruit, leaves, and bark of the daphne are poisonous.

The daylily comes in a wide variety of colors, including red, maroon, gold, yellow, and orange. Blooming season varies with variety—from early summer to late summer.

The delphinium requires a moist, well-fertilized soil, preferably alkaline. Blooms are various shades of blue, purple, pink, yellow, or white. A wonderful cut flower.

Dianthus is also known as carnation, pink, maiden pink, and sweet william. In Christian legend, the tears that Mary cried at Christ's crucifixion are said to have turned to flowers upon striking the ground; for this reason, maiden pink is sometimes referred to as "the tears of the Virgin Mary." In Italian folklore, the white carnation is associated with death and burial. Flowers are pink, white, red, or bicolor.

A popular legend links the flower of the dogwood to the crucifixion of Christ. *Cornus florida*, the most common type, produces large white or pink flowers in late spring and red berries in the summer that are relished by birds.

Fennel symbolizes resurrection and rebirth. Although an annual, fennel acts like a perennial in warmer climates.

Common Name	Botanical Name	Type	Zone	Light
fig	*Ficus*	deciduous tree (evergreen in warm climates)	7-10	full sun
flax	*Linum*	perennial	3-9	full sun
forget-me-not	*Myosotis*	biennial or annual	3-10	partial shade to shade
forsythia	*Forsythia*	deciduous shrub	4-7	full sun or partial shade
geranium	*Pelargonium*	annual (perennial in zones 9-11)	all	full sun to partial shade
germander	*Teucrium chamaedrys*	deciduous shrub	5-10	full sun
gladiolus	*Gladiolus*	flowering bulb/ annual	all	full sun

Comments

In India, it is believed that the ghosts of brahmans live in fig trees, which are sacred to the Hindus. In addition to the fig tree, there is a creeping fig, which is an evergreen vine that produces inedible fruit but is excellent for walls and hanging baskets. The weeping fig (*Ficus benjamina*) and the rubber plant (*Ficus elastica*) are both popular evergreen houseplants.

Flax produces blue or yellow flowers from May to September. It will self-sow.

In a European legend, a youth drowns picking this flower for his beloved. His last words are "Forget me not!" A 6- to 12-inch tall spreading plant with tiny, profuse, exquisite blue flowers in the spring.

Clusters of yellow flowers appear on the forsythia in early to mid spring. A vigorous and hardy plant that can be used for hedges or ground cover.

The flower clusters of the geranium are white, pink, or purple. Scented geraniums are typically brought indoors for the winter in all but the warmest climates. Vining types are great for hanging baskets.

Once established, the hardy germander requires little water and will tolerate poor soil. Purple, pink, or white flowers appear in late spring and summer.

The gladiolus blooms 60 to 100 days after planting. Its flowers are white, purple, red, yellow, or orange. An excellent cut flower.

Common Name	Botanical Name	Type	Zone	Light
globe amaranth	Gomphrena	annual	all	full sun to partial shade
hawthorn	Crataegus	deciduous tree	3-6	full sun to partial shade
holly	Ilex	evergreen shrub	6-9	full sun to partial shade
hollyhock	Alcea rosea	annual; biennial in milder zones	2-9	full sun
hyacinth	Hyacinthus orientalis	blooming bulb	all	full sun to partial shade
hydrangea	Hydrangea	deciduous shrub	3-8	full sun to partial shade

Comments

The globe amaranth symbolized immortality and unfading love in the Victorian language of flowers. White, pink, purple, orange, or red flowers appear throughout the summer.

In Celtic folklore, the hawthorn, named for its sharp thorns, is associated with ever-lasting life. It produces white flowers in the spring and red or scarlet fruit in the fall. In the fall, its leaves turn red and gold.

Holly is a traditional symbol for renewal, resurrection, and eternal life. It produces small white flowers in spring, followed, in most varieties, by bright red berries in the fall. Leaves are glossy green. Though it grows slowly, it can exceed 30 feet at maturity.

The hollyhock produces white, apricot, yellow, purple, red, pink, or maroon flowers in summer. It self-sows so easily, it is considered a perennial in some zones.

In Greek mythology, Hyacinthus was a young Spartan prince whom a jealous god killed. From his blood Apollo caused a flower to grow that supposedly displayed the Greek word for "woe" on its petals and leaves. In the Victorian language of flowers, the purple hyacinth signified sorrow. Very fragrant blooms of purple, blue, pink, cream, salmon, white, or red flowers appear in the spring.

The hydrangea produces large clusters of small flowers—white, purple, blue, or pink—in early to late summer, depending on the variety. It dies back during the winter in colder zones.

Common Name	Botanical Name	Type	Zone	Light
iris	Iridaceae	perennial	3-10	full sun
ivy	Hedera	evergreen perennial vine	5-10	full sun to shade
lamb's ear	Stachys lanata	perennial	4	full sun to partial shade
larkspur	Consolida	annual	all	full sun, with some shade in hot areas
laurel (bay)	Laurus	evergreen shrub/ perennial herb	7-10	full sun to partial shade

Comments

In Greek mythology, the goddess Iris accompanied the dead to the afterlife. The flower came to represent a link between the living and the dead and was often placed on graves. The white iris, indicating the purity of the soul, is traditionally planted on the graves of Muslims. Depending on the variety, blooms will appear from spring to early summer. The iris comes in an extraordinary range of colors.

Like many evergreens, ivy is a symbol of rebirth, immortality, and everlasting love. Ivy is also traditionally associated with healing. An effective ground cover that will hold soil on slopes, preventing erosion.

Lamb's ear—a type of stachys or betony—is a low-growing, spreading plant that produces small purplish or reddish flowers in summer. Its leaves are soft, silvery, and felt-like, hence the name. A lovely complement to pastel-colored gardens.

The larkspur can bloom throughout the growing season if sown at three-week intervals. Its flowers are blue, purple, lavender, pink, red, or white.

The ancient Greeks often used laurel, or bay, in funeral wreaths, and laurel has long been connected with death and the afterlife. An easily shaped, vigorous plant with fragrant dark leaves. Tiny white flowers appear in early summer, followed by small black berries in the fall.

Common Name	Botanical Name	Type	Zone	Light
lavender	Lavandula	perennial	4-9	full sun
lilac	Syringa	deciduous shrub	2-8	full sun to partial shade
lily	Lilium	blooming bulb	all	full sun to partial shade
lily-of-the-valley	Convallaria majalis	perennial	2-8	shade to partial shade
locust	Robinia	deciduous tree	all	full sun

Comments

The fragrant aroma of lavender has been thought to provide comfort for the grieving soul, and the plant is symbolically associated with memories and peace. The blooms are lavender, blue, violet, or purple. An excellent flower for drying.

The lilac produces remarkably fragrant clusters of small flowers in shades of purple, lavender, pink, or white, blooming in late spring to early summer. Many varieties are available. Lilac grows well in almost any soil and is often used for hedges.

The lily is a traditional symbol for death and the transition of the soul to the afterlife, so it is often used in funerals and memorials. Tombs in the ancient city of Pompei featured lilies as remembrances for the dead. In one Spanish legend, a lily grows from the heart of a devout young Christian after he is buried. Folklore has it that the soul becomes a lily upon death. Another legend tells how a lily was moved to tears for Christ in the Garden of Gethsemane; a tear remains in each bloom today, a symbol of grief and humility. Hardy lilies come in many colors; all die back after flowering.

The lily-of-the-valley is a symbol of resurrection, often specifically linked with Christ's resurrection. Extremely fragrant white or pink bell-shaped flowers appear in spring. An excellent ground cover for shady areas near buildings, fences, or trees.

The locust tree symbolized "affection beyond the grave" in the Victorian language of flowers. White or pink flowers appear in spring, followed by red or blue berries.

Common Name	*Botanical Name*	Type	Zone	Light
lupine	*Lupinus*	perennial	4-8	full sun to partial shade
marigold	*Tagetes*	annual	all	full sun
marjoram	*Origanum*	annual herb in northern zones; perennial in warmer climates	all	full sun
mint	*Mentha*	perennial herb	all	full sun to partial shade
morning-glory	*Ipomoea purpurea*	annual vine	all	full sun

Comments

The lupine grows up to 5 feet tall, with long spikes of flowers in a wide array of colors: white, cream, yellow, pink, blue, red, orange, purple, and bicolor. The blooms appear in late spring to early summer.

In some folk cultures of both Asia and Europe, the marigold has been thought to soothe a sorrowful heart. For the Victorians, the marigold symbolized grief and remembrance. Many varieties are available, from dwarf varieties to plants that can grow up to 4 feet tall. The marigold is very hardy and easy to grow. It blooms continuously throughout the growing season in shades from pale yellow to deep gold and maroon. Scented types are often used to repel garden pests.

Marjoram was planted by the ancient Greeks on graves to help the dead sleep peacefully. Sweet marjoram (*Origanum majorana*) is the most common garden species; pot marjoram (*Origanum onites*) is hardier but smaller. Grown both for its fragrance and use in cooking, marjoram can be used for border plantings.

Use caution when planting a mint; it can become very invasive. Plant where it will have boundaries, or use a pot sunk into the ground.

The twining vines of the morning-glory have large, heart-shaped leaves and blue, red, pink, white, purple, or bicolored flowers that bloom every morning once the plant is established. Be aware that the seeds of the morning-glory can become invasive.

Common Name	*Botanical Name*	Type	Zone	Light
moss, Irish	*Arenaria verna* or *Sagina subulata*	perennial	2-10	full sun to partial shade
myrtle	*Myrtus*	evergreen shrub	9-10	full sun to partial shade
nasturtium	*Tropaeolum*	annual	all	full sun to partial shade
nemophila (baby-blue-eyes)	*Nemophila*	annual	all	full sun to partial shade
oak	*Quercus*	deciduous tree	3-10	full sun
oregano	*Origanum vulgare*	perennial herb	3-10	full sun
palm	numerous genera	evergreen tree	10	full sun

Comments

"Irish moss" is the common name for two similar species: *Arenaria verna*, also known as moss sandwort, and *Sagina subulata*, also known as Corsican pearlwort. Both produce small white flowers in summer and are often used as ground cover.

The myrtle is traditionally associated with immortality. The leaves of the myrtle are fragrant when crushed. White or pink flowers appear in spring or summer; dark berries appear in the fall.

The nasturtium grows 12 to 18 inches tall, with some climbing varieties growing even taller. Its flowers come in shades of cream, yellow, orange, red, gold, and maroon.

The light-blue blooms of nemophila, or baby-blue-eyes, appear from mid-spring through early summer. The plant grows in mounds 6 to 12 inches wide and tall.

The Druids believed that the dead resided inside of oak trees. In Western culture, the acorn has traditionally been associated with immortality. A majestic, long-lived tree.

Oregano produces small lovely purple or pink flowers in summer. A beautiful but hardy plant that's easy to grow and has many culinary uses.

A palm branch was the symbol of the ancient Egyptian god of eternity, Heh. A traditional symbol of victory, the palm branch represents Christ's victory over death in Christian mythology. It is also a symbol of the Christian garden of paradise. Most types will not tolerate freezing temperatures. Often grown as a houseplant.

Common Name	Botanical Name	Type	Zone	Light
pansy	Viola tricolor	annual/biennial	all	full sun to partial shade
parsley	Petroselinum crispum	annual or biennial herb	all	full sun to partial shade
passionflower	Passiflora caerulea	evergreen or semi-evergreen vine	5-10	full sun
pearly everlasting	Anaphalis margaritacea	perennial	3-8	full sun
peony	Paeonia	perennial	2-8	full sun to partial shade
peppermint	Mentha piperita	perennial herb	all	full sun to partial shade
periwinkle	Vinca minor	evergreen perennial	4-9	partial shade to full shade

Comments

The name "pansy" comes from the French *pensee* for thoughts or remembrance. From the same genera (*Viola*) as the violet, the pansy is ideal for borders, rock gardens, and spring-flowering bulb gardens.

For the ancient Greeks, parsley was a symbol of death that was often used in funeral wreaths. It is a compact plant, good for edging.

The passionflower is a vigorous vine that can grow up to 20 feet in length. Large white flowers tinged with pink or lavender appear in summer. Popular in the South, some cold-resistant varieties are available as well.

The pearly everlasting prefers a moist, rich soil. It blooms in late summer. Its button-like flowers are pearly white; its foliage is gray-green. A good cut flower. Also, a good dried flower for winter arrangements.

The peony has traditionally been considered a healing plant. Its large, exceptionally fragrant flowers can be white or one of many shades of red. The peony blooms from mid-spring into early summer and requires little care.

Peppermint has invasive qualities. Use caution where you plant it, or plant it in a pot and sink the pot into the ground

Periwinkle produces lavender-blue flowers in summer on trailing vines. A spreading ground cover, good for slopes or shady areas, but potentially quite invasive.

Common Name	Botanical Name	Type	Zone	Light
persimmon	*Diospyros*	deciduous tree	6-10	full sun
phlox	*Phlox*	perennial	2-10	full sun to partial shade
pine	*Pinus*	coniferous tree or shrub	3-10	full sun
plum	*Prunus mume*	deciduous tree	3-10	full sun
poppy	*Papaver*	perennial or annual	all	full sun

Comments

In the Victorian language of flowers, the persimmon signified "Bury me amid nature's beauties." Although *Diospyros virginiana* is native to the Southeastern United States, the persimmon tree is rarely cultivated here. Also called "possumwood" because possums like to feast on persimmon fruit.

Phlox produces flowers in shades of magenta, white, lavender, pink, or red. Creeping phlox is a hardy, low-growing plant with needle-like foliage—an excellent ground cover for slopes. Larger varieties grow up to 4 feet tall. All are easy to cultivate.

In China, the pine tree symbolizes the triumph of virtue over adversity and the eternal cycle of life and death. In Western cultures, it is associated, along with evergreens generally, with everlasting life. Some pine trees can grow over 100 feet tall. Smaller pines, like the dwarf mugo, are good for foundation plantings or as specimen plants.

In China, the plum symbolizes hope and rebirth. There are many varieties, with varying degrees of hardiness. The dwarf varieties are better suited for most gardens.

Garlands of poppies were placed on mummies in ancient Egypt. Ancient Greeks also crowned their dead with poppies. In Europe, legend has it that poppies spring up on battlefields from the blood of slain soldiers, hence their association with veterans of wars. The poppy symbolized consolation, sleep, and rest in the Victorian language of flowers and was commonly used to memorialize the dead. The oriental poppy (*Papaver orientale*) produces striking flowers in a rainbow of colors in early summer. The alpine poppy (*Papaver alpinum*) is good for rock gardens and retaining walls.

Common Name	*Botanical Name*	Type	Zone	Light
primrose	*Primula*	perennial	3-5	partial shade; won't tolerate extreme heat or cold
purple coneflower	*Echinacea*	perennial wildflower	3-9	full sun to partial shade
rhododendron (azalea)	*Rhododendron*	deciduous or evergreen shrub	3-8	full sun to partial shade
rose	*Rosa*	perennial shrub	3-10	full sun to partial shade
rosemary	*Rosmarinus officinalis*	perennial herb	6-11	full sun

Comments

In Greek mythology, primrose was called "paralisos" for the son of Flora and Priapus, who died mourning the death of his betrothed. The primrose was given to the earth by Flora and Priapus as a living memorial to their son. Because it symbolized sadness in the Victorian language of flowers, primrose was often planted on the graves of children. Colors include pink, red, scarlet, purple, white, yellow, and lavender.

The hardy purple coneflower produces large purple flowers on stalks up to 4 feet tall from summer into fall. The flowers attract butterflies; birds are drawn to the seed heads after the petals fall off.

Rhododendron is a large family that includes the azaleas. Rhododendrons are prized for their profuse blooms of rose, crimson, white, orange, scarlet, red, yellow, pink, salmon, violet, bicolor, and mixed color flowers.

The belief that only a single red rose can pass with a human soul from this world to the next is quite ancient. The Egyptians decorated their tombs with roses, and in more modern times, roses have traditionally been placed or dropped on graves. In Christian legend, a rose with eight petals represented resurrection or rebirth. Roses come in many colors, sizes, and types, including hybrid tea roses, floribundas, grandifloras, miniatures, and climbing roses. An incomparable cut flower.

Rosemary is a traditional symbol of remembrance, as Ophelia remarks in Shakespeare's *Hamlet*. The herb has highly aromatic leaves and small lavender-blue or white flowers that appear in early spring.

Common Name	Botanical Name	Type	Zone	Light
rudbeckia (coneflower)	*Rudbeckia*	perennial	3-9	full sun to partial shade
rue (herb of grace)	*Ruta*	perennial herb	4-10	full sun to partial shade
sage	*Salvia officinalis*	perennial or annual herb	all	full sun
shasta daisy	*Chrysanthemum maximum*	perennial	4-10	full sun to partial shade
snowdrop	*Galanthus*	blooming bulb	all	full sun to partial shade
spruce	*Picea*	evergreen tree	2-8	full sun to partial shade
sunflower	*Helianthus*	annual	all	full sun

Comments

The daisy-like rudbeckia, or coneflower, grows 2 to 3 feet tall, with yellow or orange flowers that have cone-shaped cores. A good cut flower.

Rue, also known as herb of grace, is a shrub-like perennial with aromatic blue-green leaves and small yellow-green flowers. It is sometimes used to repel insects.

Sage was considered to have healing properties in ancient Greek culture. It has been used for centuries for both medicinal and culinary purposes.

The shasta daisy is a vigorous plant that produces an abundance of beautiful white blooms throughout the summer. An excellent cut flower.

The snowdrop is a traditional emblem of death in Christian mythology. During the Renaissance, the hanging head of the flower was used to represent the Virgin Mary's sorrow over Christ's crucifixion. The three inner petals of the flower are said to look like a death shroud. In the Victorian language of flowers, the snowdrop symbolizes hope. White bell-shaped flowers appear in early spring.

Be mindful of the eventual size of the spruce when placing it in your landscape. Some varieties grow only 5 to 6 feet tall; others grow as tall as 150 feet.

The sunflower is a symbol of remembrance and rebirth. Some varieties reach 10 feet, with flower heads that can exceed a foot in width. The colors of the flowers include yellow, orange, gold, and bicolor. Leave seed heads on to attract birds.

Common Name	Botanical Name	Type	Zone	Light
sycamore	*Platanus*	deciduous tree	5-10	full sun
thrift	*Armeria maritima*	perennial	3-9	full sun; some shade in warmer climates
tulip	*Tulipa*	blooming bulb	4-8	full sun to partial shade
vibernum	*Vibernum*	deciduous shrub	2-10	full sun to partial shade
violet	*Viola*	perennial/ annual	3-5	partial shade

Comments

In ancient Egypt, sycamores were believed to form the eastern gate of heaven and were often planted near tombs or used as wood for coffins. These large trees provide excellent shade.

The thrift symbolized sympathy in the Victorian language of flowers. Rose-pink or white flowers appear in late spring and last into summer. Good for rock gardens and edgings. Also known as sea pink.

In Islam, the tulip is a traditional symbol for the death of a martyr. Tulips come in many colors: red, yellow, white, pink, lavender, purple, and cream. A wonderful cut flower.

The vibernum, or cranberry bush, produces long-lasting pink or white fragrant blooms in late spring to early summer, followed by red or black berries in the fall. The fruit is very attractive to birds.

In Greek mythology, Ajax committed suicide when he failed to avenge his friend Hector's death. Where his blood dropped on the ground, violets appeared—a living tribute to their friendship. The Romans used violets to decorate tombs. In Christian legend, violets were white until the crucifixion of Christ, when, to reflect Mary's grief, they turned purple—a color traditionally associated with mourning. Blue, purple, rose, or white flowers complement the deep green foliage of the heart-shaped leaves on this charming low-grower. The fragrant flowers bloom in early spring.

Common Name	*Botanical Name*	Type	Zone	Light
walnut	*Julgans*	deciduous tree	5-8	full sun
willow, weeping	*Salix babylonica*	deciduous tree	5-8	full sun
yarrow	*Achillea*	perennial	3-8	full sun
yew	*Taxus*	evergreen shrub	3-7	full sun to partial shade

Comments

The walnut tree is traditionally associated with funerals. The slow-growing black walnut (*Juglans nigra*) does not make a good lawn tree because its roots emit toxins that can damage surrounding plants. Plant in pairs for better nut production.

As is the case with many "weeping" plants, the weeping willow is a traditional symbol for mourning. In Celtic folklore, the willow was associated with death. This graceful pendulous tree grows well in wet areas.

The yarrow is traditionally associated with healing. Its fern-like foliage forms an attractive background for clusters of bright white, yellow, pink, or red flowers that bloom from summer through fall. In addition to attracting butterflies, it makes a great cut or dried flower.

In Celtic folklore, the yew symbolized death, rebirth, and immortality. It was placed on graves as a reminder that death is but a transition to a new life. In the Victorian language of flowers, the yew symbolized sorrow. The needles of the yew are about an inch long, dark green, and lustrous. Red berries ripen in the fall. A fine foundation plant that can be easily shaped.